Iona Abbey
Worship Book

Iona Abbey
Worship Book

The Iona Community

wild goose
publications  www.ionabooks.com

Contributions copyright © the individual contributors
Compilation copyright © The Iona Community 2016

Published 2017, reprinted 2017, 2018 and later
Wild Goose Publications
Suite 9, Fairfield, 1048 Govan Road, Glasgow G51 4XS, Scotland
the publishing division of the Iona Community.
Scottish Charity No. SC003794. Limited Company Reg. No. SC096243.

ISBN 978-1-84952-513-8

Cover photo © David Coleman

The publishers gratefully acknowledge the support of the Drummond Trust, 3 Pitt Terrace, Stirling FK8 2EY in producing this book.

All rights reserved. Apart from the circumstances described below relating to non-commercial use, no part of this publication may be reproduced in any form or by any means, including photocopying or any information storage or retrieval system, without written permission from the publisher (via PLSclear.com).

Non-commercial use: The material in this book may be used non-commercially for worship and group work without written permission from the publisher. If photocopies of small sections are made, please make full acknowledgement of the source, and report usage to the CLA or other copyright organisation.

The Iona Community has asserted its right in accordance with the Copyright, Designs and Patents Act, 1988, to be identified as the author of this work.

Overseas distribution
Australia: Willow Connection Pty Ltd, Unit 4A, 3–9 Kenneth Road, Manly Vale, NSW 2093
New Zealand: Pleroma, Higginson Street, Otane 4170, Central Hawkes Bay

Printed by Bell & Bain, Thornliebank, Glasgow

Contents

Preface		7
1A	Welcome Service A	9
1B	Welcome Service B	15
IC	Appendix to Welcome Services	19
2A	Sunday Morning Communion Service A	23
2B	Sunday Morning Communion Service B	35
2C	Appendix to Sunday Morning Services	45
3A	Service of Quiet A	53
3B	Service of Quiet B	57
3C	Appendix to Services of Quiet	59
4A	Morning Service	63
4B	Morning Service – All-age	71
4C	Appendix to Morning Services	77
5A	Leaving Service	85
5B	Leaving Service – All-age	89
6A	Service for Justice and Peace A	93
6B	Service for Justice and Peace B	97
6C	Appendix to Services for Justice and Peace	103
7A	Service of Prayers for Healing A	109
7B	Service of Prayers for Healing B	115
7C	Appendix to Services of Prayers for Healing	121
8A	An Act of Commitment A	129
8B	An Act of Commitment B	133
8C	Appendix to Acts of Commitment	137

9A	Ceilidh Communion	147
9B	A Ceilidh Service	153
9C	Appendix to the Ceilidh and Ceilidh Communion Services	157
10A	Creation Liturgy	165
10B	Appendix to Creation Liturgy	169
11A	Evening Liturgy	175
11B	Appendix to Evening Liturgy	181
12A	Prayers for the World and Its People	187
12B	Appendix to Prayers for the World and Its People	191

Psalms	197
Chants	251
Short songs suggested for the liturgies	264
Concerning worship	266
The Iona Community	268

Preface

The Iona Community believes that worship is more than a religious service in a consecrated building. We believe that in all we do, we are – or should be – honouring the Maker of heaven and earth in whose image we are made.

At the centre of our faith is the affirmation that God not only made the world, but loved and loves the world. This is witnessed to in the Hebrew and New Testament scriptures and is celebrated, endorsed and epitomised in the incarnate life of Jesus. His ministry was not primarily to the religious establishment of his day, but to and for the world. And it was sometimes to the distress of the pious that he highlighted the significance to God of marginalised people – particularly women, the poor and the abused – and matters of public and private practice regarding issues such as money, race, and what makes for peace and reconciliation.

This belief is affirmed in the way visitors to the Community's centres on Iona share meals, engage in daily work and conversation, and at the beginning and end of each day gather for a service of worship, most frequently in the rebuilt Benedictine Abbey Church. These services follow a pattern, initiated by George MacLeod the founder of the Iona Community, which has developed over the years. The morning service from Monday to Saturday has a set liturgy similar to a daily office, but distinct in its form and substance. Each evening service is devoted to a different aspect of faith and discipleship in which we affirm that the concerns of the world and its people must always be allied to the will of God.

This is the fifth substantial *Iona Abbey Worship Book*. As with its predecessors, it includes new initiatives and developments of past patterns of worship. Most of the services are offered in two versions, allowing variety for those regularly leading or engaging in worship on Iona. The liturgies may either be used as written or be amended to suit the occasion. Each section of liturgies is followed by an appendix which offers alternative or supplementary resources.

Most of the liturgies require the leader to prepare an introduction as part of the gathering time. This ensures that all have some understanding of what we do and why we do it, as well as getting a sense of what they are about to participate in. Written introductions also preface most of the liturgies and it is hoped that people may have time to read these before the service begins. It is not intended that they be read aloud. The gathering time also includes the teaching of songs.

As previously, there is a selection of psalm texts which are used primarily in the daily morning services. These are not literal translations, but in many cases are paraphrases developed from a variety of translations to make the ancient texts accessible.

The *Iona Abbey Worship Book* was compiled by members of the Iona Community in consultation with staff working on Iona and members who regularly visit the island centres. It is offered to people of faith and doubt whose presence is always valued on Iona, and offered to God in gratitude for a legacy which began in 563AD when St Columba landed on the island, and which, we pray, will last for many years to come.

The Iona Community
Epiphany 2017

Winter variations in Iona Community worship services

In the winter, when there are only a few guests and visitors and a small group of staff, there are fewer services and they are held in the more intimate and marginally warmer Michael Chapel.

The Morning Service, with its associated cycle of prayers and psalms, is observed as usual, though at a slightly later time. Instead of holding the Communion Service in the Abbey church on a Sunday morning, members of the Resident Group join islanders in the Parish Church, and share with them in the leading of worship.

Sunday evening quiet time is also an ecumenical event. The only other evening services in the Michael Chapel are on Tuesday – the service of prayers for healing – and on Thursday – a communion or agapé.

1A Welcome Service (A)

The people gather

Welcome, introduction and conversation

Gathering song/s

Responses

Leader Gathered together –
the familiar and the unknown,
residents and visitors,
for the first time or the umpteenth time,
All come, Holy Spirit.

Gathered together –
where Celtic saints and Benedictine monks worshipped,
where raiders and reformers ransacked,
where pilgrims and puzzled people have prayed,
where God has listened,
come, Holy Spirit.

Gathered together –
not knowing what we have in common,
not sure, perhaps, why we are here,
unable to read God's mind,
come, Holy Spirit.

To open doors, dispel fears,
establish friendships,

reveal what is in us,
and bring us closer to Christ,
**come, Holy Spirit.
Meet us here.**

Song

Prayer

Leader   You, God, have brought us to this thin place
where earth and heaven embrace,
the past interweaves with the future,
different nations and languages mingle,
and what we want is replaced by what we need.

All   **God, you are good to us.**

And if we feel strange
because this place and those around us are unfamiliar;
and if we feel tired
because we have travelled far;
and if we feel uncertain
because we do not know what is before us,
still let us gladly say:
God, you are good to us.

Bless those we have left behind,
reveal your wisdom through those we meet,
rest your peace on what weighs heavily on our hearts;
and plant your purpose in what we deeply desire,
so that when we leave we can say with truer conviction,
**God, you are good to us.
Amen.**

The lighting of lights

Leader	We light a light in the name of the Maker, who shaped the world and laid his hand on us.
All	**Gloria, gloria, gloria, in excelsis Deo** *(sung repeatedly as a candle is lit)*
Staff & Islanders	We light a light in the name of the Son who lit the world and breathed the breath of life for us. **Iona Gloria** *(as above)*
Visitors	We light a light in the name of the Spirit who encompasses the world and blesses our hearts with yearning **Iona Gloria** *(as above)*

**We light three lights
for the Trinity of love,
God above us,
God beside us,
God within us,
the beginning,
the end,
the everlasting one.**

Scripture readings *(see appendix for selection of possible readings)*

Silence

Prayer

Leader   Into your care, O God,
we place those whom we love …
those for whom we worry …
those from whom, in time or place or affection,
we are distant …

(pause)

Into your care, O God,
we place what grieves us …
… and what inspires us and fills us with hope …

(pause)

Into your care, O God,
we give ourselves …

(pause)

Leader   God bless to us our bodies,
All   **God bless to us our souls,
God bless to us our lives,
God bless to us our belief.**

Leader   Let us share the prayer that Jesus taught us
in our own language or preferred version.

**Our Father in heaven,
hallowed be your name;
your kingdom come,
your will be done on earth as in heaven.
Give us today our daily bread;
and forgive us our sins
as we forgive those who sin against us.**

**Save us in the time of trial
and deliver us from evil;
for the kingdom, the power and the glory
are yours,
now and for ever.
Amen.**

Song

Closing responses

Leader   May the blessing of light be upon us:
All   light without and light within.

> May the moon, sun and stars shine on us
> and warm every heart
> till it glows like a great fire
> so that strangers and friends
> may come in and find welcome.
>
> **May light shine out from our eyes
> like a candle set in a window.
> And may God bless us
> with goodness and loving kindness.
> Amen.**

1B Welcome Service (B)

The people gather

Welcome, introduction and conversation

Chant

Opening responses

Leader	At the close of this day we gather to worship God;
All	**at journey's end we give thanks** **for the road travelled and the open door.**
	We offer to God our tiredness and our expectancy; **we rejoice in a God who welcomes us just as we are.**
	Here and now we might entertain angels unaware; **here and now we can meet Christ in one another.**

Song of praise

Call to prayer *(remain standing)*

Leader	God of creation, of the stars and the tides,
All	**hear our prayer.** God-with-us, Jesus our brother, **hear our prayer,** Spirit of pilgrimage, gathering us together **hear our prayer.**

Prayer *(sit or kneel)*

Leader	Loving God, here we are, your children, at the end of a journey and the beginning of a week.

For some of us this ancient place is strange and amazing;
for others it has become home.

Some of us are uncertain of what lies ahead;
and others are eager to explore.

Some of us have brought burdens we need to lay down;
others are looking for challenges to take up.

Here we are, your children,
with our unique stories,
different needs, varied gifts.

All **Help us to learn here that we are loved,
and to celebrate the humanity we share.
Amen**

The lighting of lights

Voice A At journey's end,
as the sun sets in the west,
and granite glows with evening light,
between these sheltering walls
we light a candle
for the Maker of earth and sky,
of day and night:
a sign of faith.

All **Gloria, gloria, gloria,
in excelsis Deo** *(sung repeatedly as a candle is lit)*

Voice B In this place of welcome,
doors are opened,
lights shine from the windows;
and among companions
we light a candle
in the name of Jesus

who came to share our human lives:
a sign of love.
Iona Gloria *(as above)*

Voice C   In the darkest night
stars still shine;
on an island out at sea
we are not alone;
so we light a candle
to celebrate the Spirit
bringing encouragement:
a sign of hope.
Iona Gloria *(as above)*

Scripture reading *(see appendix for selection of possible readings)*

Silence

Prayer

Leader   In the light of your love, O God,
we acknowledge the many things on our minds,
and the concerns that we carry with us.

(silence)

Free us from the grip of busyness and worry;
help us to put any anxiety into your hands.

(silence)

Enable us to be open to the healing and humour
and hope of the coming week.
And, while we are here, we commit to your care
those we name in our hearts.

(silence)

Now, grateful that we are free to unite in prayer,
we pray in words Jesus taught his friends:

(in our own language or preferred version)

All **Our Father in heaven,**
hallowed be your name;
your kingdom come,
your will be done on earth as in heaven.
Give us today our daily bread;
and forgive us our sins
as we forgive those who sin against us.
Save us in the time of trial
and deliver us from evil;
for the kingdom, the power and the glory
are yours,
now and for ever.
Amen.

Song

Blessing & response

Leader As we share this place and time,
All **may our life in community**
reflect the dance of the Trinity
by which the world is blessed.

The blessing of God,
Our Maker, Befriender and Inspirer,
be with us all.
Amen.

1C Appendix to Welcome Services

NOTES FOR THE SERVICE

1) Conversation

This service begins with a conversation initiated by the leader who encourages the congregation to greet each other and discuss their answer to a question. This question has to be one to which everyone can respond, irrespective of age, intellect or familiarity with the congregation – for example, 'What memory do you bring from last week to the coming week?' There is no 'feeding back'. Music may call people back together.

2) The lighting of the lights

Each of the welcome services involves the lighting of three candles, each lighting being followed by the singing of the Iona Gloria.

With a smaller congregation, the candles may be placed on the communion table or somewhere central, and lit during the Glorias. With a larger congregation it may be preferable to have large candles already lit, but hidden from sight. Then during the singing of the Glorias these can be carried to bases in different areas of the church, such as the chancel, crossing and nave. Only one candle is lit or carried per section of the text.

If candles are to be carried through the Abbey church this action should be rehearsed in advance.

EXTRA RESOURCES

Suggested gathering songs

God Welcomes All
Come All You People
In the Lord, I'll be ever thankful
Know that God is Good (Mungu ni mwema)
Laudate Omnes Gentes

Opening words (a)

Leader A   This is a place where saints were found
a special house, a holy ground
where scripture, song and fervent prayer,
work and discussion, food and care
have shaped the heritage we share.

All   **This is a place for God.**

Leader B   This is a space where saints are grown
as faith is shared and love is shown,
where all who doubt or who believe
are asked to give and to receive
and share with Christ the air we breathe.
This is a space for God.

Leader C   This is a time of fond surprise
for hearts and minds and ears and eyes,
where what's gone wrong can be forgiven
and what's to come is glimpsed or given
as earth makes room for more of heaven.
This is a time for God.

Leader D   This is a place and space and time
for paths to walk and hills to climb,

for us to find a better view
of all that's good and just and true
and let God's Spirit make all new.
This is the place for us.

Opening words (b)
(an ancient Celtic rune of hospitality)

Leader   We saw a stranger yesterday.
All   **We put food in the eating place,
drink in the drinking place,
music in the listening place.**

And, in the sacred name of the triune God,
he blessed us and our house,
our cattle and our dear ones.
**As the lark says in her song:
often, often, often goes the Christ
in the stranger's guise.**

Suggested scripture readings:

Abraham and Sarah entertain angels	Genesis 18:1-8 (& 9-15)
Elijah and the widow	1 Kings 17:1-16
Elijah in the wilderness	1 Kings 19:1-8
Jesus and the children	Mark 9:33-37
	Mark 10:13-16
Jesus with Martha and Mary	Luke 10:38-42
Jesus and Zacchaeus	Luke 19:1-9
The Emmaus road	Luke 24:13-35
The Church as the joined-up body	1 Corinthians 12:12-26
Loving fellow Christians	Hebrews 13:1-2
	and other verses

Closing prayer

Leader   Stay with us, Lord,
since the day is far spent and night is coming.
Kindle our hearts on the way
that we may recognise you in the scriptures,
in the breaking of bread,
and in each other.
All   **Amen.**

Blessing

Leader   The blessing of Martha's welcome,
the blessing of Mary's listening,
the blessing of action,
the blessing of reflection,
the blessing of God,
be with us all.
All   **Amen.**

2A Sunday Morning Communion Service A

The people gather

Every Sunday morning we share an ecumenical service of worship which includes the sacrament of Holy Communion. The order of worship is not drawn from any particular denomination and seeks to be as inclusive as possible.

To this end, children are welcome among us and have the option of leaving after the first prayer for their own activities in the Chapter House. They will return when the offering is being taken. Irrespective of their age, if they and their parents are willing, they may partake of Holy Communion. The sacrament is open to all and will be shared in the following way:

(Either)

1) *The bread and wine will be brought from the table to the seated congregation and passed from hand to hand. Anyone who does not wish to partake should simply pass the elements from the neighbour on one side to the neighbour on the other.*

(Or)

2) *The bread and wine will be brought to two or three stations in the church and people will be invited forward to receive. If you are sitting in a row that ends next to a wall, please step back to allow those closest to the wall to receive communion first, thus enabling an easy return to the seats.*

Should anyone prefer to receive a blessing, they should simply bow their head before the person serving the bread.

We normally use fermented wine and bread made from wheat. Those wishing gluten-free bread and non-alcoholic wine will be directed to a specific place in the Abbey church.

During worship, an offering is taken for the work of the Iona Community here and on the mainland.

Welcome, notices and introduction

Opening responses

Leader With nature in its power and beauty,
with rain and wind and sunshine,
with the ancient rocks and the budding flower,
All **we gather in praise of God.**

With believers and seekers the whole world wide,
with people in every land,
and speakers of every language,
we gather in praise of God.

With the angels and saints in heaven,
with Columba who built community here
and with all who have worshipped in this place,
we gather in praise of God.

With Jesus who promised his presence
and the Spirit who showers her blessings,
we gather in praise of God.

Here let heaven and earth embrace;
here may God's people find home.

Song or hymn

Call to prayer *(remain standing)*

Leader Eternal God, Maker of the skies above,
lowly Christ, Lover of the earth and its people,
unfettered Spirit, Giver of gracious gifts,
All **you are present among us.**

O hidden mystery,
sun behind all suns,
soul within all souls,
in all we touch, in all we meet,
you are present among us.

As bearers of your image,
we come to be reshaped;
dependent on your mercy,
we ask to be made new.

(all sit or kneel)

Prayer

Leader   For the right roads we avoided travelling,
and the kindly words we refused to share;
for the false gods who received our worship
and the true selves we have starved of love …
God, by your grace,

All   **forgive us.**

For the hidden hurts we have held too tightly,
and the promises which we never kept;
for the careless use of our time and money
and the lame excuses we should never have made,
God, by your grace,
forgive us.

(pause)

For all we should be
and all we can amend,
God, in your love,
renew us.

For all you have in store for us
and all you may demand of us,
God, in your love,
prepare us.

For the life of the world
and the love of its people,
God, in your love,
commit us.

(Sung or spoken)
Kyrie eleison *(God have mercy on us)*
Christe eleison *(Christ have mercy on us)*
Kyrie eleison *(God have mercy on us)*

Hear and believe these words of Jesus:

Your sins are forgiven.
Go in peace.
Come and follow me.

(pause)

Glory to the Creator who gives us life,
Glory to Jesus whose love remakes us,
Glory to the Spirit, companion on our journey.
Glory be to God. Amen.

(Children may leave now for their own programme in the Chapter House, to return later during the offering.)

Reading

(when other than the Gospel)
Leader   Listen for God's word
coming to us in Scripture.
All   **Our hearts and minds are open.**

(reading)

Reader God be in our listening,
 God in our understanding.
 Amen

Leader *(when the Gospel)*
 We greet the Gospel of Jesus the Christ
 by standing to sing Alleluia.

 (an Alleluia is sung, followed by the reading)

Reader This is the Gospel of Christ.
 Amen! Thanks be to God.

Song

Sermon or reflection

Affirmation of faith

All **We believe in God above us,
 Maker and Sustainer of all life,
 of sun and moon,
 of water and earth,
 of male and female.**

 **We believe in God beside us,
 Jesus Christ, the Word made flesh,
 born of a woman, servant of the poor,
 tortured and nailed to a tree.
 A man of compassion, he died forsaken;
 he descended into the earth
 to the place of death.**

**On the third day he rose from the tomb;
he ascended into heaven
to be everywhere present;
and his kingdom will come on earth.**

**We believe in God within us,
the Holy Spirit of Pentecostal fire,
life-giving breath of the church,
spirit of healing and forgiveness,
source of resurrection and eternal life.
Amen.**

Prayers of concern

Leader Let us pray.

Maker and Lover of all,
in the mystery of your kindness
you have bound us to each other,
and called us to serve the earth and its people.

So hear us, as in this ancient place of worship
we pray for the churches to which we belong
that they may ever be centres of faith, hospitality
and imagination,
modelling the future rather than lamenting the past.

(pause)

God, in your mercy,

All **hear our prayer.**

Grateful for the life in our bodies,
we pray for those whose lives are diminished
by ill health, depression, grief or rejection,
asking for the healing, the affirming, the listening

which will encourage and restore them.

(pause)

God, in your mercy,
hear our prayer.

Conscious of the peace of this place,
we pray for those who have no peace
because of war or the fear of war,
or the threat of violence,
or the grip of hunger,
or the loss of hope.
May the voice of the victims be heard
and the work of the peacemakers be blessed.

(pause)

God, in your mercy,
hear our prayer.

Surrounded by rugged and tender beauty,
we pray for the earth,
especially where it is damaged by human carelessness
and threatened by human greed;
and ask that we may learn to care for the earth as you do.

(pause)

God, in your mercy,
hear our prayer.

And because we are here to meet with Jesus,
we join our words to those he taught us, saying

(in our own language or preferred version)

Our Father in heaven,
hallowed be your name;
your kingdom come,
your will be done on earth as in heaven.
Give us today our daily bread;
and forgive us our sins
as we forgive those who sin against us.
Save us in the time of trial
and deliver us from evil;
for the kingdom, the power and the glory
are yours,
now and for ever.
Amen.

The offering

Leader We continue our worship in the giving of our offering.

Communion song

Offering prayer *(remain standing)*

Celebrant All that we have and all that we are
are God's gifts to us.
So here we return a token of our wealth
asking that it and all we possess be used to God's glory.
All **Blessed be God for ever.**

The invitation *(remain standing)*

The story *(all sit)*

The Eucharistic prayer

Celebrant	The Lord be with you
All	**and also with you.**
	Lift up your hearts.
	We lift them up to God.
	Let us give thanks to God our Maker.
	It is right to give our thanks and praise.

(a prayer follows, leading into)

Sanctus *(spoken or sung)*

All	**Holy, holy, holy God of power and might, heaven and earth are full of your glory. Hosanna in the highest!**
	Blessed is the One who comes in the name of the Lord. Hosanna in the highest!
Celebrant	Because you, gracious God, have been faithful to us, we will be faithful to Jesus.
	He promised to be with those who met in his name:
All	**this we believe.**
	He promised to hear the prayers of faithful people:
	this we believe.
	He said that in the communion of bread and wine he would be present to us as we remembered him:
	this we celebrate.

So, send now your Spirit among us
and upon this bread and wine,
that we may taste and see your goodness,
be embraced by your love,
and be engaged in your service.
Amen.

As Jesus did, so we do.
We break this bread
   (the bread is broken)
We share this wine
   (the cup is raised)
We believe that he who lived,
died and rose again for us
will meet us here.

Graciously nourish us, O Christ,
so that we who try to follow you
may receive food for the journey
and be bound in solidarity
with all who walk in your way.
Amen.

Agnus Dei *(may be said or sung)*

All   **Lamb of God, you take away the sin of the world, have mercy on us.**

   Lamb of God, you take away the sin of the world, have mercy on us.

   Lamb of God, you take away the sin of the world, give us your peace.

Celebrant   Take this bread, share this wine.

In these Christ comes to us
with love
from God.

The gifts of God
for the people of God.

The Communion

The peace

(peace is shared by all with the words)
Peace be with you.

Prayer

Celebrant	Give thanks for all God's goodness:
All	**God's love shall last for ever.**

Generous and faithful God,
you have fed us at your table.
May the nourishment we have received
enable us to enrich the lives of others
wherever we may go from here.

Whether the future be dark or bright,
the road be smooth or rough,
whether our cares be light or heavy,
our song be strong or weak,
keep our hearts warm
and our hands open,
our lives ever embracing
and ever embraced by your love.
Amen.

Blessing

Celebrant May the everlasting God shield you
wherever you go.

And the blessing of God be upon you
All **the blessing of the Giver of life.**

The blessing of God be upon you
the blessing of the Christ of love.

The blessing of God be upon you
the blessing of the Spirit of peace.

The blessing of the Trinity be upon you
now and evermore.
Amen.

Closing song *(during which the Communion elements are processed out of the Abbey church)*

(Before the closing song, this may be announced:
Following the service, everyone is invited to have tea or juice in the cloisters. As you leave the church, you will be given a small oatcake and be invited to share it with a stranger. This tradition enables us to continue our celebration together in the place of the common life.)

2B Sunday Morning Communion Service B

(You may read more about this service on pages 23-24)

The people gather

Welcome, notices and introduction

Opening responses

Leader Thanks be to you, O God, that we have risen this day
to the rising of this life itself.
The purpose of God be between us and each purpose,

All **the hand of God between us and each hand;**
the pain of Christ between us and each pain,
the love of Christ between us and each love.

O God, you brought us to the light of this new day;
bring us to the guiding light of eternity.

Song

Call to prayer *(standing)*

Leader We gather in God's name;
we claim Christ's promised presence.

My sisters and brothers,
not out of dread and fear,
but believing in the understanding and forgiveness
of God,
let us rid ourselves of what we need to carry no longer.

(all sit or kneel)

Prayer of confession and restoration

Leader Let us pray

Eternal Maker of the endless heavens,
lowly Christ, befriender of the changing earth,
Holy Spirit, wind over the flowing waters,
in earth, sea and sky
you are ever present.

All **O hidden mystery,
sun behind all suns,
soul within all souls,
in everything we touch,
in everyone we meet
you are there,
and we give you thanks.**

But where we have not touched but trampled you
in creation,
where we have not honoured but avoided you
in one another,
where we have not received but rejected your goodness,
forgive us,
and hear our plea for your pardon.

Holy God,
**holy and mighty,
holy and immortal,
have mercy on us.**

Or *(sung response)*
Kyrie eleison *(God have mercy on us)*
Christe eleison *(Christ have mercy on us)*
Kyrie eleison *(God have mercy on us)*

Leader	Know that God is good,
	and that to those who are truly sorry
	God forgives what is past
	and enables us to begin again.

Once we were no people,
now we are God's people.
Once we were beyond God's mercy;
now that mercy has been given to us.

So let us live
as those who treasure God's costly generosity,
by safeguarding God's earth,
delighting in its people,
and loving our Maker
to whom be glory for ever.
Thanks be to God.
Amen.

Reading

(when other than the Gospel)
Leader Listen for God's word
coming to us in Holy Scripture
All   Our hearts and minds are open.

(reading)

Reader God be in our listening,
God in our understanding.
Amen

(when the Gospel)
Leader We greet the Gospel of Jesus the Christ
by standing to sing Alleluia.

(an Alleluia is sung and the Gospel is read)

Reader This is the Gospel of Christ.
Amen. Thanks be to God.

Song

Sermon or reflection

Affirmation of faith

All **We believe in God,**
Who conceived all that is created,
God, who fathers and mothers all people.

We believe in Jesus Christ
God's firstborn and only Lord of the earth.
He came from both heaven
and the womb of the virgin Mary;
he lived in solidarity with humankind,
befriending, teaching,
healing and restoring;
he was denied and betrayed by his friends;
and was done to death by the state.
He descended to the place of oblivion,
rose to life again on the third day,
and ascended to heaven
where he sits at God's right hand.
This same Jesus will come again in glory
to judge the living and dead.

We believe in the Holy Spirit,
whose dynamic presence can make all things new.
And we believe in the holy catholic church,
the communion of saints,
the forgiveness of sins,

> **the resurrection of the body
> and the life everlasting.
> Amen.**

Prayers of concern

Leader Holy God,
who, in Jesus, touched the earth,
admiring its beauty and blessing its people,
we honour you for the gift of life
and all the gifts that life brings us:
food, shelter, company,
the experiences that make us think,
the people that bring out the best in us.

Hear our prayers for the places in this world
where beauty has turned to ugliness,
food has been replaced by famine,
friendship has been forgotten
and fear, hostility and hopelessness
have the upper hand.

(pause)

God, in your mercy,

All **bring healing, bring peace.**

Hear our prayers for people who cannot pray
because of pain, loss or worry;
and for those who will not love themselves
and so cannot love their neighbour.

(pause)

God, in your mercy,
bring healing, bring peace.

Hear our prayers for ourselves –
our private yearnings,
our secret hopes
and any doubt, jealousy or anger
to which we hold too tightly.

(pause)

God, in your mercy,
bring healing, bring peace.

And hear us as we, in our mother tongue,
say the words Jesus first prayed in his.

**Our Father in heaven,
hallowed be your name;
your kingdom come,
your will be done on earth as in heaven.
Give us today our daily bread;
and forgive us our sins
as we forgive those who sin against us.
Save us in the time of trial
and deliver us from evil;
for the kingdom, the power and the glory
are yours,
now and for ever.
Amen.**

The offering

Communion song

The invitation

The story

Prayer of thanksgiving

Celebrant	The Lord be with you.
All	**And also with you.**
	Lift up your hearts.
	We lift them up to God.
	Let us give thanks to God.
	It is right to give our thanks and praise.

For you, Creator God,
the valleys laugh and sing
and the trees of the field clap their hands.

Your earth summons us to break silence
and be one with the song of creation.
We give you thanks and praise

For you, God of all,
the church in its myriad forms
and countless languages honours its Saviour.

Millions upon millions invite us
to be one with them in the drama of worship.
We give you thanks and praise.

In heaven, beyond our seeing,
the angels and saints are caught up in song.
And those we have loved and lost
are part of that great company.

They call us to be one with the harmony of heaven.
We give you thanks and praise.

So, gladly, we join our voices
to those of earth, sea and sky,
in the universal hymn of praise
which echoes through time and eternity.

Sanctus *(may be spoken or sung)*

**Holy, holy, holy God of power and might,
Heaven and earth are full of your glory.
Hosanna in the highest!**

**Blessed is the One who comes
in the name of the Lord.
Hosanna in the highest!**

Prayer of consecration

Come now, O Christ,
bone of our bone, flesh of our flesh,
forever bound to us in promise and mystery;
breathe your Spirit on us
and on this bread and wine.
Let them become, for us,
the seal and sign of your love
healing, redeeming, making us whole.

And through them let us together become, for you,
your body,
loving the world as God loves,
serving its people as God wills
and always being transformed
until we and all humanity
resemble the One whose food we now share.

As Jesus broke bread,
we break this bread.

(bread is broken)

As Jesus shared wine
we share this cup.

(cup is raised)

Agnus Dei *(may be spoken or sung)*

> **Lamb of God, you take away the sin of the world,
> have mercy on us.**
>
> **Lamb of God, you take away the sin of the world,
> have mercy on us.**
>
> **Lamb of God, you take away the sin of the world,
> give us your peace.**

Celebrant   As those who have been invited to his table,
feed on this holy food
through which God comes to us
so that we can come to God.

Communion

The peace *(... shared by all with the words)*

> **Peace be with you**

Prayer

Celebrant O Brother Jesus,
we have been guests at your table;
come with us wherever we go
and be present in all we share.

All **Summon out in us, whom you have fed,
generosity of spirit
to ensure that all the hungry are nourished
and earth's barren places are fertile
with food, faith, hope and love.
Amen.**

Blessing

Celebrant Now go in peace,
do what God wills,
follow where Christ calls,
pray for the gifts of the Spirit;
and may the blessing of God
the Creator, Redeemer and Sustainer
rest on and remain with you
now and always.
Amen.

2C Appendix to Sunday Morning Services

EXTRA RESOURCES

The Apostles' Creed

All　　We believe in God, the Father almighty,
　　　　Creator of heaven and earth.

　　　　We believe in Jesus Christ, his only Son, our Lord,
　　　　who was conceived by the power of the Holy Spirit
　　　　and born of the virgin Mary.
　　　　He suffered under Pontius Pilate,
　　　　was crucified, died and was buried.
　　　　He descended to the dead.
　　　　On the third day he rose again;
　　　　he ascended into heaven
　　　　and is seated at the right hand of the Father.
　　　　He will come again to judge the living and the dead.

　　　　We believe in the Holy Spirit,
　　　　the holy catholic church,
　　　　the communion of saints,
　　　　the forgiveness of sins,
　　　　the resurrection of the body
　　　　and the life everlasting.
　　　　Amen.

Affirmation of faith *(all-age)*

All **We believe in God.**
Child Tell me about God? What does God do?
Voice A God makes the stars and spiders.
Voice B God is warm and bright and full of colour.
Voice C God is our friend – who loves us
and calls us by name.

All **We believe in Jesus.**
Child What is he like? Tell me about him.
Voice A He was exciting.
Voice B He told lots of stories.
Voice C He listened to people – he made them think.
Voice A Some people didn't like Jesus.
They told lies about him.
He was sentenced to death and killed.
Voice B But God brought Jesus
back to life again.
Voice C Following Jesus is an adventure – a journey
– a good surprise.

All **We believe in the Holy Spirit.**
Child Tell me about her? What does she do?
Voice A She helps us remember what Jesus said.
Voice B She lets us know how much God loves us.
Voice C She helps us to love other people.
Voice A She's someone we can't see but feel
Voice B like the wind blowing in our hair
Voice C like the warmth of a candle flame.

All **We believe in the Church.**
Child This church here?

Voice A	Every church, all of them together.
Voice B	Not the buildings, but all the people who love God.
Voice C	All of us working together with God to make the world beautiful.
All	**We believe God calls us.**
Child	To do what?
Voice A	To love all people.
Voice B	To forgive them when they hurt us.
Voice C	To trust and not be afraid.
Voice A	To help make the world the place God wants it to be.
Voice B	To care for the world and enjoy it.
Voice C	Amen
Child	Pardon?
Voice A	Amen – it means so be it, OK, let it happen.
Child	Oh, OK – Amen.
All	**Amen**

***

The invitation (service A)
(Congregation standing at this point)

Celebrant	We are here because Jesus has called us – strangers and friends, locals and visitors, believers and doubters, the certain and the curious. It is always a mixed company that Jesus gathers and invites to his table where, in bread and wine, he meets us

and through him we, who are different,
are joined to each other.

So come,
not because you understand,
but because you are understood.

Come,
not because of how you feel,
but because God has food for you.

Come,
not because you deserve a place,
but because Jesus invites you,
just as you are.

(Congregation invited to sit)

The story (service A)

Celebrant   This sacrament began
on the night of Jesus' arrest,
when he and his disciples gathered round a table.

Reader   During their meal, Jesus took bread,
and when he had blessed it,
he broke it and said,
'This is my body. It is given for you.
Do this to remember me.'

Later he took a cup of wine,
and when he had blessed it he said,
'This cup is the new relationship with God
made possible because of my death.
Drink it, all of you, to remember me.

| | I shall not share this with you again
until I do so in God's coming kingdom.' |
|---|---|
| Celebrant | So now we do as Jesus did and commanded us to do.
We take this bread and wine,
the ordinary things of the world which Christ,
in his own way, will make special,
and as he said a prayer before sharing
we do so too. |

The Eucharistic prayer (service A)

Celebrant	The Lord be with you
All	**and also with you.**
	Lift up your hearts.
	We lift them up to God.
	Let us give thanks to God our Maker.
	It is right to give God thanks and praise.

Praise is yours, holy God …
praise beyond all telling.
All that we are, all that we have,
all that we know and all that is yet to be
comes from your care.

Water and wisdom,
light and longing,
the stones in the earth
and the hope in our hearts
are grounded in your graciousness.

The life of the world and all its people,
nature and human skill
celebrate you as first mover
and final destiny.

Therefore, to the unending song
of earth, sea and sky
we join our praise.

To the anthems of the company of heaven –
the angels and archangels,
the saints of every age –
we join our praise.

And as one with your people on earth,
north and south, east and west,
we join our praise,
singing the song of your eternal greatness.

Sanctus *(return to page 31 for Sanctus and consecration)*

The peace

Celebrant Not an easy peace,
not a conditional peace,
not a half-hearted peace,
but the peace of Christ
is with us now.

Let us share it with each other.

***

The invitation (service B)
(The congregation remains standing)

Celebrant This table does not belong to any denomination,
church or community.
It belongs to Jesus.

It was at table that he met people,
heard their stories and shared his.
It was at table that he deepened his friendship
with poor folk and prostitutes,
the business class and puzzled bystanders.
It was at table that he shared profound insights
into who God is and what God wants.

And it was at table, with bread and wine,
that he initiated the sacrament we now celebrate.

So come to this table.
Leave behind any baggage of arrogance or unworthiness.
Do not think, 'This is not for me.'
Think rather of Jesus saying, 'I am for you,'
and accept his invitation to be the friend
he cherishes and longs to feed.

(The congregation is invited to sit)

The story (service B)

Reader   Long before this building was erected
in open spaces and hard places
people heard of how on the night of his arrest,
and aware of what lay ahead of him,
Jesus sat at supper with his friends.

During the meal, he took a piece of bread,
blessed and broke it
and said to his disciples,
'This is my body, given for you.'

Later in the meal he took a cup of wine, saying,
'In this cup is the new relationship with God

| | made possible because of my death.
Drink it, all of you.' |
|---|---|

> I will not drink wine again until I do so
> in the coming kingdom of God.

| Celebrant | So we take this bread and this wine
offering them to God for blessing
so that through them the goodness of God
may bless, enrich and enlighten us. |
|---|---|

The peace (service B)

| Celebrant | Angels said it to frightened shepherds,
Jesus said it to dismayed disciples.
And now these words which come from heaven
are given to reconcile us to God and to each other. |
|---|---|
| | Peace be with you |
| **All** | **and also with you.** |
| | Let us share this peace with each other. |

(Notes for those serving bread:
People will have been instructed that if they wish to receive a blessing, rather than bread and wine, they should bow their head before the person serving the bread. In this instance, the server should give a simple blessing, such as, 'God bless you and keep you.')

3A Service of Quiet A

The people gather

Every Sunday evening we come together not so much to share words as to share silence. We do this because God is as present in silence as in speech. The silence will last for around twenty minutes.

This will be followed by a brief prayer for others and for members and associates of the Iona Community who are remembered on this day of the month. After the service concludes, people may leave quietly or stay in the Abbey church, which will remain lit for a short while.

Opening prayer

Leader Jesus,
you commanded waves to be still
and calmed a stormy sea.
Quieten now our restless hearts
that they may find rest in you.

We recognise the noise inside us
and the noises around us.
We acknowledge them,
but seek here to know your presence
in the midst of all that might distract us.

So, now, we surrender for these moments our speech,
knowing that beneath the silence is a deeper Word,
and that even when we say nothing,
you are still listening.

Prayer

Leader   Ever listening,
ever watchful,
ever loving God,

All   **we rest in you.**

Ever listening,
ever watchful,
ever loving God,
we rest in you.

Silence

Prayers for others

Leader   Holy God,
as you have heard every silent prayer
and wordless petition,
hear now these prayers for others.

*(Any prayers the leader may offer
will end with the following response:)*

God, in your mercy,

All   **hear our prayer.**

*(Then follows a prayer for members of the Iona
Community and their families and associate members,
as remembered on specific days of the month.)*

(This is followed by:)

Leader   Walk with them today, O God,
and keep us on your way.

Words of sending

Leader May you be out of your depth –
as the deeps of the night sky
contain but cannot explain God's mystery.

May you be in the dark –
as the moon is eclipsed, but held safe,
with all that is, in the palm of God's hand.

May you be lost for words –
as the Word is spoken
in the silence of the night,
in the beauty of God's creation.

The loving blessing of God,
Creator,
Healer,
and Holy Spirit,
be in us and around us tonight,
tomorrow,
and all our nights and days.

All **Amen.**

3B Service of Quiet B

The people gather

There are some brief words of introduction to this service on page 53.

Opening prayer

Leader   God within and beyond us all,
teach us the silence of humility,
> the silence of wisdom,
> the silence of love,
> the silence of faith,
> the silence that enables reflection
> and speaks without words.

> Teach us, God, to silence our own hearts and minds
> that we may listen
> for the movement of your Spirit within us,
> and treasure your presence
> in the depths of our being.

Silence

Prayers for others

Leader   Holy God,
as you have heard every silent prayer
and wordless petition,
hear now these prayers for others.

*(Any prayers the leader may offer
will end with the following response:)*

	God, in your mercy,
All	**hear our prayer.**

(Then follows a prayer for members of the Iona Community and their families and associate members, as remembered on specific days of the month.)

(This is followed by:)

Leader	Walk with them today, O God,
	and keep us on your way.

Blessing

Leader	May God be
	a bright flame before you,
	a guiding star above you,
	a smooth path below you,
	a kindly shepherd behind you,
	tonight and tomorrow and for ever.
All	**Amen.**

3C Appendix to Services of Quiet

Notes for the service

These words spoken by the leader may be helpful in introducing this service.

> In this evening's service, we turn from sound and action
> to silence and stillness.
> There will be 20 minutes of silence
> (which may begin and end with the sound of a bell or a chime).
> Our time will close with a spoken prayer.
>
> Many of us live active and busy lives
> and our minds and hearts reflect that busyness.
> In this service we take the opportunity to be still together.
> Rather than focusing on God as beyond or above us,
> we turn our attention to God who dwells within each of us.
>
> Spending time with God in quiet
> is not an escape from the troubles of the world,
> for the God we encounter is also at the heart
> of the world's life and struggles.
>
> So, now, as we move into silence,
> let us ensure we are sitting comfortably,
> our backs upright and supported.
> We may wish to close our eyes,
> uncross our legs and breathe normally,
> as we become quietly alert to God's presence.

After the opening prayer, there may be a few words leading into the silence, from the Bible or from the sacred writings of other faith traditions, such as those printed below in the extra resources section.

EXTRA RESOURCES

We may reflect on these words as we make our way into the silence:

1. Go carefully when you visit the house of God. Do not be impulsive in speech, nor be guilty of hasty utterance in God's presence. God is in heaven, you are on earth, so let your words be few. *(Ecclesiastes 5:1-2)*

2. The quieter you become, the more you are able to hear.
   (Rumi)

3. O Great Spirit, help me always to speak the truth quietly, to listen with an open mind when others speak, and to remember the peace that may be found in silence.
   (Cherokee prayer)

4. Let nothing disturb you; let nothing dismay you;
   all things pass; God never changes.
   Patience achieves all that it strives for.
   Those who have God find they lack nothing;
   God alone is enough.
   (Theresa of Avila)

5. There is nothing so much like God in all the universe as silence.
   (Meister Eckhart)

6. God was not in the wind that shattered the rocks, nor in the earthquake, nor in the fire. After the fire there was a faint murmuring sound. When Elijah became aware of it, he wrapped his face in his cloak and went out to stand at the entrance of the cave. There came a voice: 'Why are you here?'
   (1 Kings 19:12-13)

Marking the silence

The leader may choose to mark the beginning and ending of the period of silence with a sound such as a bell, chime or singing bowl.

Prayers for others

These prayers should be short and include immediate concerns for the world and the prayers for the day in the Iona Community's prayer diary, including concerns and prayers for members and associates.

Prayer

Leader For silence in the evening
we give you thanks.

For listening to our questions
we give you thanks.

For wonder and tears
we give you thanks.

For laughter and mystery
we give you thanks.

For you being you and for us being us
we give you thanks.

All **Amen.**

Nunc dimittis

The prayer recorded in Luke's Gospel as spoken by Simeon after he had seen the Christ child.

Leader   Now, O God,
         may your servants go in peace
         as you promised,
         for our eyes have seen the salvation
         which you have prepared for all to see:
         a light to enlighten the nations
         and the glory of your people.
All **Amen.**

4A Morning Service

The people gather

Welcome and notices

Opening responses *(standing)*

Leader	The world belongs to God,
All	**the earth and all its people.**

How good it is, how wonderful
to live together in unity.

Love and faith come together;
justice and peace join hands.

If Christ's disciples keep silent,
these stones would shout aloud.

Open our lips, O God,
and our mouths shall proclaim your praise.

Song of praise

Call to prayer *(standing)*

Leader	Move among us, God; give us life;
All	**let your people rejoice in you.**

Give us again the joy of your help;
with your spirit of freedom sustain us.

God, make our hearts clean,
restore us in body, mind and spirit.

Let us pray

Prayer of confession *(sit or kneel)*
(here the leader may offer a brief prayer)

Leader Trusting in God's forgiveness,
let us in silence confess our failings
and acknowledge our part in the pain of the world.

Silence

Leader Before God,
with the people of God,
I confess to turning away from God
in the ways I wound my life,
the lives of others
and the life of the world.

All **May God forgive you, Christ renew you,
and the Spirit enable you to grow in love.**

Leader Amen.

**Before God,
with the people of God,
we confess to turning away from God
in the ways we wound our lives,
the lives of others
and the life of the world.**

Leader May God forgive you, Christ renew you,
and the Spirit enable you to grow in love.

Amen.

The Lord's Prayer

Leader So now, as Jesus taught us, we say:

All	Our Father in heaven,
	hallowed be your name,
	your kingdom come,
	your will be done on earth as in heaven.
	Give us today our daily bread;
	and forgive us our sins
	as we forgive those who sin against us.
	Save us in the time of trial
	and deliver us from evil;
	for the kingdom, the power
	and the glory are yours,
	now and for ever.
	Amen.

Response of faith *(standing)*

Leader	With the whole church
All	**we affirm**
	that we are made in God's image,
	befriended by Christ,
	empowered by the Spirit.
	With people everywhere
	we affirm
	God's goodness at the heart of humanity
	planted more deeply than all that is wrong
	With all creation
	we celebrate
	the miracle and wonder of life,
	the unfolding purposes of God
	for ever at work in ourselves and the world.

Psalm *(as announced)*

The reading

Leader   Listen now in the reading of scripture for the word and wisdom of God.

(reading

... followed by a silence, at the end of which the leader says:)

Leader   For the Word of God in scripture,
for the Word of God among us,
for the Word of God within us,
thanks be to God.

Song

(On Friday mornings we move to page 85 at this point to continue with the leaving service.)

Prayers of gratitude and concern

*(Any prayers the leader may offer
will end with the following response:)*

Leader   God, in your mercy,
All   **hear our prayer.**

(Then follows a prayer for members of the Iona Community and their families and associate members, as remembered on specific days of the month.)

(This is followed by:)

Leader   Walk with them today, O God,
and keep us on your way.

Daily prayers

Monday

Leader   God, in whose heart is love and justice,
show us this day whom we must love
and what we should challenge or change
in order that your will for the earth might be done.

All   **Increase our hope,
dispel our apathy;
inspire our imagination,
and deepen our commitment
until we become the signs of your kingdom
for which we and others pray.
Amen.**

Tuesday

Leader   O Christ, the Master Carpenter,
you at the last, through wood and nails,
crafted our whole salvation.

All   **Wield well your tools
in the workshop of your world,
so that we who come rough-hewn to your bench
may here be fashioned
to a truer beauty of your hand.
Amen.**

Wednesday

Leader   O God, you gave to your servant Columba
gifts of courage, faith and cheerfulness,
and sent out your servants from Iona
to carry your Gospel to every creature.
Grant we pray a like spirit to your church
even at this present time.

	Further in all things the purpose of this community, that hidden things may be revealed to us and new ways found to touch the hearts of all.
All	**May we preserve with each other sincere charity and peace; and, if it be your holy will, grant that this place of your abiding continue still to be a sanctuary and a light. Amen.**

Thursday

Leader	Jesus, you have set before us a great hope that your kingdom will come on earth, and have taught us to pray for its coming.
All	**Make us ready to celebrate the signs of its dawning, and to pray and work for the perfect day when your will shall be done on earth as it is in heaven. Amen.**

Friday

Leader	O Christ, you are within each of us. It is not just the interior of these walls, it is our own inner being you have renewed. We are your temple not made with human hands; we are your body.

**If every wall should crumble,
and every church decay,
we are your habitation.**

Nearer are you than breathing,
closer than hands and feet.
Ours are the eyes with which you, in the mystery,
look out with compassion on the world.

**So we bless you for this place,
for your directing of us,
your redeeming of us,
your presence among us.**

Take us outside, O Christ, outside holiness,
to where nations clash at the crossroads of the world.

**So shall this building continue to be justified;
and your people find cause
to bless your name.
Amen.**

Saturday

Leader Ever-present God, set your blessing on us
as we begin this day together.
Confirm in us the truth by which we rightly live;
confront us with the truth from which we wrongly turn.

All **We ask not for what we want
but for what you know we need,
as we offer this day and ourselves
for you and to you.
Amen.**

Silence

Closing responses *(standing)*

Leader   This is the day that God has made;
All   **we will rejoice and be glad in it.**

We will not offer to God
offerings that cost us nothing.

Go in peace to love and to serve;
we will seek peace and pursue it.

In the name of the Trinity of Love,
God in community, holy and one.

(We remain standing to leave, our worship continuing in our work and all we do today.)

4B Morning Service – All-age

This order of worship is intended for occasions when there is likely to be a number of children or families in the congregation or groups for whom English is not their first language. The pattern is similar to that of the main morning service, but the language is simpler and more accessible.

The people gather

Welcome and notices

Opening words *(standing)*

Leader	The world belongs to God,
All	**the earth and all its people**

(a large globe is brought forward)

It is good to live in community,
to work and talk with each other
(a tea-towel is brought forward)

Love and faith come together;
justice and peace join hands
(a Bible is brought forward)

If the friends of Jesus keep silent,
these stones would shout aloud
(a handful of stones is brought forward)

We are glad to be in God's house,
to listen and sing and pray
(a lit candle is brought forward)

Morning song

Saying sorry *(sitting)*

Leader God you know me.
You know that I can be loving and kind;
and you know that sometimes I get things wrong.
I'm sorry for the times I hurt other people,
forget to listen to you
and don't bother to take care of your world.

All **May God forgive you,
Jesus bless you,
and God's Spirit help you to grow in love.**

Leader Amen.

All **God you know us.
You know that we can be loving and kind;
and you know that sometimes
we get things wrong.
We're sorry for the times we hurt other people,
forget to listen to you
and don't bother to take care of your world.**

Leader May God forgive you,
Jesus bless you.
and God's Spirit help you to grow in love.

All **Amen.**

The Lord's Prayer

Leader   We say together the prayer which Jesus taught his friends:

All   **Our Father in heaven,
hallowed be your name,
your kingdom come,
your will be done on earth as in heaven.
Give us today our daily bread;
and forgive us our sins
as we forgive those who sin against us.
Save us in the time of trial
and deliver us from evil;
for the kingdom, the power
and the glory are yours,
now and for ever.
Amen.**

Saying yes

Leader   Because God cares for us,
All   **we will care for each other.**

           Because we are part of God's creation,
           we will care for the earth.

           Because we are loved by God,
           we will share God's love with everyone.

(On Friday mornings we move to page 89 at this point to continue with the leaving service.)

Psalm

A reading or story

Leader   For words that tell stories,
for words that make us laugh and cry,
for words that make us think,
All   **Thank you God.**

Song

Thank you prayers and prayers for other people

(A brief prayer of thanks
A prayer for a situation in the news
A prayer for countries in the world
A prayer for members and associates of
the Iona Community
This is followed by:)

Leader   Walk with them today, O God,
All   **and keep us on your way.**

Prayer for today

Leader   It's a new day.
Twenty-four hours of it.
Time to go for a walk.
Time to do the washing-up.
Time to ask questions.

Time to think and be quiet.
Time to try something new.

It's a new day.
Walk beside us God.
Enjoy the day with us.
We want to share it with you.
Amen.

Silent prayer *(we are quiet for a moment to say our own prayers)*

Closing words *(standing)*

Leader   This is the day that God has made:
we will rejoice and enjoy it.

Today we will share with God
everything that is important to us.

Go in peace and be kind.
Today we will help those around us.

Go in the name of God,
God who loves us for ever.

(The objects which were brought in during the opening responses are now carried from the Abbey and the congregation follows behind them.)

4C Appendix to Morning Services

EXTRA RESOURCES FOR SERVICE 4A

Examples of prayers that may be used before the confession

a) Generous God,
   this day and all its possibilities
   are your gifts to us.
   Make us ready to receive your grace
   this morning and every morning.

b) Into the wonder of this new day
   we come, as we are, to God,
   bringing with us
   our hopes, our fears, our stories.

c) God of the morning,
   God of life,
   we come to enjoy your company;
   we are here to seek your truth.

d) Maker of All,
   because you delight in your creation,
   and love each of us with equal cherishing,
   we pause to honour your name
   and to examine ourselves in the light of your love.

Examples of prayers that may be used to begin prayers of gratitude and concern

a) In this moment, here among us,
God is listening,
God is loving,
God wants to know what is in our hearts.

So, God,
we bring to you our gratitude for love and beauty
and kindness …

and we bring our concern for your people and your world …

b) Living Word, we give thanks for words –
spoken and read –
which encourage, inspire, challenge
and help to build community.
We remember in our prayers the different needs
of your children who yearn to hear good news …

of those who stop their ears to the cries of the world …

and those whose voices are silenced …

c) Gathering God
we give thanks for the vision, adventure and passion
that have brought us together
in this place.
Help us to be open today …
   grateful to meet Jesus in each other,
   happy to do a new thing,
   thankful for the space to be.
Help us to be open to the possibilities it gives us
for our life in community beyond this place.

d) Creator God,
this place fills our hearts with joy:
the blues and greys of sea and sky,
the music and voices echoing within these walls,
the diversity of the people around us;
your divine imagination delights and surprises us –
may it always be so.
Wherever we find ourselves,
may we also find you.

EXTRA RESOURCES FOR SERVICE 4B

Psalms for all-age morning service

Psalm 19:1-6

A   The sky shows us God's glory;
it shows us what God has made.

B   The sun comes out in the morning
like a bride and bridegroom full of joy.

A   The sun comes out in the morning
like an athlete eager to run a race.

B   The sun starts at one end of the sky
and moves across to the other.

A   The sun is full of light;
nothing can hide from its heat.

B   Without words, the sky speaks of God's glory;
it shows us what God has made.

Psalm 19:7-11,14

A   God tells us how to behave.

B   God shows us what is right.

A   God teaches us to be fair.

B   God gives us wisdom and strength.

A   God's truth is more precious than gold.

B   God's wisdom is sweeter than honey.

All   **May our thoughts and words make God smile. May our actions make God happy.**

Psalm 104

A   God, you are big and strong;
you are beautiful and full of light.

B   You use the clouds as your chariot;
you ride on the wings of the wind.

A   You made the earth with its mountains;
you spread out the seas like a velvet cloak.

B   The trees get plenty of rain,
and in them the birds build their nests.

A   Lions roar in the darkness;
badgers hide in the cliffs.

B   Sea monsters play in the oceans,
and ships sail on the seas.

A   God, you have created so many things.
    May you be happy with what you have made.

**All We will always sing songs to God.
    May God enjoy our singing.**

Psalm 139

**All You know me, God.
    You know me.**

A   You see me working;
    you see me resting.

B   You know what I think about;
    you know what I do.

A   You are everywhere –
    near and far,
    and all around me.

B   You are in the light,
    and in the darkness too.

A   You knew me before I was born;
    you know how long I will live.

B   Your knowledge is amazing, God;
    no one is as wise as you.

A   Take a long look at me, God;
    see the good and the bad in me.

B   Let your love grow and grow in me
    and guide me along your way.

Psalm 147

A   It is good to sing to God.

B   It is fun to sing and make music.

A   God gives each star a name.

B   God is in the wind and frost.

A   God makes the grass grow on the hills.

B   God gives the animals their food.

A   God comforts those who are sad.

B   God cares for those who need a home.

A   God enjoys the love of friends.

B   God gives us our daily bread.

SHORT STORIES AND POEMS SUITABLE FOR ALL-AGE MORNING SERVICE

The Lion Storyteller Bible – Bob Hartman
A Day's Work – Eve Bunting
In God's Name – Sandy Eisenberg Sasso
Dogger – Shirley Hughes
Slowly, Slowly, Slowly, Said the Sloth – Eric Carle
Dinosaurs and All That Rubbish – Michael Foreman
Wilfrid Gordon McDonald Partridge – Mem Fox
Jesus' Day Off – Nicholas Allan
The Bird – Nicholas Allan
Rainbow Crow – Nancy Van Laan
The Great Kapok Tree – Lynne Cherry
Henry's Song – Kathryn Cave & Sue Hendra
A Child's Garden – Michael Foreman
A Tapestry of Tales – Sandra Palmer & Elizabeth Breuilly
Head, Body, Legs – Won-Ldy-Paye & Margaret Lippert.
Jam – Margaret Mahy
*Washing Up – Michael Rosen
*The Creation – James Weldon Johnson
*Great, Wide, Beautiful, Wonderful World – William Brighty Rands
*Mrs Malone – Eleanor Farjeon
*Good Hope – Benjamin Zephaniah

*poem

ALTERNATIVE PRAYER FOR THE DAY

Leader Jesus, our friend,
you have promised
always to be with us.

Help us to be
loving and kind,
and to make friends,
not enemies.

All **Be with us today
and every day.
Amen.**

5A Leaving Service

Depending on the time of the ferries, this service may be contracted by singing a psalm in place of a hymn, rather than reading a psalm.

This service begins as the regular Morning Service on page 63 and diverts to these pages after the singing of the second song on page 66.

Prayers of gratitude and concern

Leader   Let us pray.
For the roots and purpose of this Community
and for all the communities of which we are a part,

All   **thanks be to God.**

For all we have shared together here
and all we can now share with others,
thanks be to God.

For the path that lies before us
and our future in God's hands,
thanks be to God.

(Here the leader offers a short prayer of gratitude, followed by prayers for:
- *the needs of the world*
- *concerns of the Iona Community.*

Each prayer ends with the words:)

Leader   God, in your mercy,
All   **hear our prayer.**

(Then follows a prayer for members of the Iona Community and their families and associate members, as remembered on specific days of the month.)

(*This is followed by:*)

Leader Walk with them today, O God,
and keep us on your way.

The Friday prayer

Leader O Christ, you are within each of us.
It is not just the interior of these walls,
it is our own inner being you have renewed.
We are your temple not made with human hands;
we are your body.

**If every wall should crumble,
and every church decay,
we are your habitation.**

Nearer are you than breathing,
closer than hands and feet.
Ours are the eyes with which you, in the mystery,
look out with compassion on the world.

**So we bless you for this place,
for your directing of us,
your redeeming of us,
your presence among us.**

Take us outside, O Christ, outside holiness,
to where nations clash at the crossroads of the world.

**So shall this building continue to be justified;
and your people find cause
to bless your name.
Amen.**

Silence

Parting blessing *(all stand)*

Those staying	God guide your feet and minds today; may you travel safely and find companions on the way.
Those leaving	God be in your hands and hearts today when you wave goodbye and prepare to welcome others.
Those staying	God be in your lives as you travel on and at your homecoming.
Those leaving	God be with you always, constant companion, guardian, friend and guide.
All	**May God's blessing be ours on our pilgrim way, all the nights and days of our journey home.**

(We remain standing and leave the church together.)

5B Leaving Service – All-age

This service begins as the regular All-age Morning Service on page 71 and diverts to these pages after the 'Saying Yes' responses on page 73.

Psalm 121

A   Where does our help come from?

B   It comes from God who made heaven and earth.

A   God doesn't go to sleep and forget us.

B   God is always awake.

A   God loves us and looks after us.

B   God guards us day and night.

A   When we go out God is with us.

B   When we come home God is by our side.

All   **God is always with us,
for ever and ever and ever.**

A reading, a story or an action

Leader   For words that tell stories,
for words that make us laugh and cry,
for words that make us think,
All   **thanks be to God.**

Song

Thank you prayers and prayers for other people

Leader For the story of the Iona Community,
and for the communities we belong to,
All **thank you God.**

For everything we have shared here,
thank you God.

For new roads to explore,
and for new things to discover,
thank you God.

(These prayers follow:
  – A prayer for a situation in the news
  – A prayer for countries in the world
  – A prayer for members and associates of
    the Iona Community

This is followed by:)

Leader Walk with them today, O God,
and keep us on your way.

Friday prayer

Leader God of the morning
wake us up.
All **Wake us up to new adventures.**
Wake us up to be kind and loving.
Wake us up to care for your world.
Amen.

Closing responses and blessing

Those leaving	For some of us it's nearly time to go, God, and soon we'll be travelling to all sorts of different places.
Those staying	Some of us will be staying here, enjoying Iona and getting ready to meet new people who will be arriving soon.
All	**Coming or going, God, you are always with us.**
Those leaving	You meet us in the lives of family and friends and strangers.
Those staying	You share our stories and our bread.
All	**Coming or going, God, you are always with us. Thank you. We are glad.**

Blessing

We ask your blessing, God,
on our lives,
our homes,
our journeys.
Wherever we rest,

wherever we travel,
bless us with love and wonder,
every day.
Amen.

(The items that were carried in at the beginning of the service are collected, processed through the nave and left on the font for the congregation to pass as they leave.)

6A Service for Justice and Peace A

The people gather

In this and the following service we draw on that part of the Iona Community's Rule which is a commitment to justice, peace and the integrity of creation.

We celebrate that God wills for the world peace with justice, known in the Middle East as 'Shalom' or 'Salaam'. This is not an abstraction or something only possible in another world or eternity, but a real hope for this place and time. This justice is proclaimed by the Law and the Prophets, and is embodied in Jesus. It flows from the simple fact that God loves the world. When what God loves is threatened, those who love God cannot remain neutral.

Welcome and introduction

Opening responses

Leader   Just and merciful God, you speak through the prophets, challenging us to seek peace rooted in justice.
All   **Help us to hear your urgent call.**

> Loving God, in Jesus you change our lives for good, challenging us to work for reconciliation.
> **Help us to see your way of truth and love.**

> With-us God, your Holy Spirit moves us to action, challenging us to live the Good News.
> **Help us to respond wholeheartedly,**
> **here and now – to say Yes!**
> **Amen!**

Song

Prayer

Voice A   Let us pray.

>Just and merciful God,
>we glimpse your presence in the world you have created,
>its power and its beauty, music and poetry,
>its diversity, fertility, the possibility of food for everyone,
>the dream of fullness of life for all your children:
>Yes, God, you are with us in this world.

Voice B   Yet we see that power misused, beauty marred,
discord and lies dividing humankind,
failure to share,
causing many to go hungry or die.
Where are you, God?

Voice A   We hear the Good News that Jesus brought,
the affirmation of the value of every human life,
the Gospel that commands us to seek peace with justice;
we understand that costly reconciliation is at its heart:
Yes, God, you are with us in this world.

Voice B   Yet we see that good news denied by apathy,
mocked by prejudice, hatred and refusal to forgive,
and we feel helpless in the face of suffering.
Where are you, God?

All   **You are present where women and men of good will
still choose to live in your way,
caring for creation and for each other,
courageously speaking truth to power.**

You are there when elderly people share their wisdom.
You are there when street children dance in the rain.
You are present wherever, in this broken world,
hope is alive.

Thank you, God, for being present with us now.
Amen.

Readings for challenge and reflection

(which should include scripture and may also include contemporary reports and creative expression)

Response

(which may take various forms to enable intercessory prayer)

Affirmation of faith *(optional)*

All We believe in God
in whom is power and compassion.

We believe in the Creator
who gave birth to the universe,
set solar systems dancing in space,
shaped molecules and mountains,
and conceived beauty beyond our imagining.
God's power topples tyrants,
and brings down walls of separation;
God's love embodies the tenderness
of a mother and father,
encouraging and caring for each of us.

We believe in Jesus,
born in obscurity in an occupied land;

a human being, vulnerable to hunger, thirst,
persecution and grief.
He understood the power of love
and confronted the powers of evil,
spoke the truth with courage and clarity,
forgave his enemies and changed lives.
In his living, dying and rising again
he showed love strong enough to save the world.

We believe in the Holy Spirit
who sustains, comforts and empowers us,
opens the scriptures, opens our minds,
and illuminates earth's darkness.
Amen.

Song

Blessing and dismissal

All May the God of Peace inspire us,
may the God of Justice empower us,
may the God of Hope encourage us
to live the Good News.

Leader Go, in the power of the Spirit.
Go, and do not try to separate politics and prayer.
Go, not to escape, but to engage with God's world.
Go, to live hopefully, as people of resurrection.
Amen

Chant/short song *(as all leave)*

6B Service for Justice and Peace B

The people gather

In this and the previous service we draw on that part of the Iona Community's Rule which is a commitment to justice, peace and the integrity of creation.

We celebrate that God wills for the world peace with justice, known in the Middle East as 'Shalom' or 'Salaam'. This is not an abstraction or something only possible in another world or eternity, but a real hope for this place and time. This justice is proclaimed by the Law and the Prophets, and is embodied in Jesus. It flows from the simple fact that God loves the world. When what God loves is threatened, those who love God cannot remain neutral.

Welcome and introduction

Opening responses

Leader O God, who created the heavens and stretched them out,
All **we praise you!**
You made the earth and all that lives here:
we praise you!
You give breath to all creatures
and your Spirit to your people:
we praise and thank you, O God!
That the eyes of the blinded be opened,
  the poor hear the good news,
  the captives be brought out of darkness,
  the wealth of the world serve the good of all,
your kingdom come, O God;
your will be done!

Then let us sing God a new song.
With joy let us honour our Maker.

Song

Prayer

Leader   Let us pray.

Over time, over space, over matter, over thought,
you are our God, in all and through all.

The noises of war are loud in your ears,
as is the cry of a newborn child.
You share the excitement of those pioneering research
as well as the last breaths of those nearing death.

And in Christ, all the pain and potential in the world
are held together in the hope of healing.

Be present to us here, gracious God,
and let your Spirit open us to glimpse that fairer world
which you intend for us and for all people.

All   **Amen**

Readings for challenge and reflection

(which should include scripture and may also include contemporary reports, drama and use of other media)

Response

(which may include symbolic action and this or another prayer)

Leader	Creator of this world and all its people, we are glad that all things are held in your hands. You have not left us alone.
	And we celebrate the work of your Spirit encouraging people the world over to work for justice and peace, to speak for the voiceless and always to anticipate that the best is yet to come.
All	**Blessed be your name.**
	If, however, we have driven a wedge between piety and peacemaking, erected a wall between prayer and politics, associated the purposes of heaven with only the gentler things of earth – God of justice, **show yourself.**
	If we have offered to false gods the devotion you alone deserve; if we have dismissed the Gospel as irrelevant to the world – God of justice, **show yourself.**
	If we have dumbed down your Word and domesticated your Spirit because we wanted an easier faith and a tamer dove – God of justice, **show yourself.**

Wherever in our nations
the poor are endangered,
the sick are neglected,
prisoners are refused redemption,
and strangers among us are suspected –
God of justice,
show yourself.

Wherever in our world,
the lust for profit
undermines the longing for peace;
or the greed for power
overrides the need for fairness –
God of justice,
show yourself.

In the prison visitor
and the mediator,
in vigils for peace
and protests to protect the earth;
to all who fear for the future of children,
to those who long for a different day –
God of justice,
show yourself.

We pray in Jesus' name
and in the power of the Holy Spirit.
Amen

Song

Blessing

Leader May God our maker bless us
and wrap us round
in love and tenderness.

May Jesus our brother bless us
and ask us the questions
that lead us to do justice.

May the Holy Spirit bless us
and fill our lives
with her courage and wisdom.

May we live bravely in the love of the Trinity
all our nights and days.

All **Amen.**

6C Appendix to Services for Justice and Peace

NOTES FOR THE SERVICE

Both orders of worship are frameworks that can be amended rather than liturgies that must be followed to the detail. As with the Commitment service, there is opportunity for people to reflect on the scripture as it is followed by poetry, testimonies, drama or symbolic action.

Rather than have a general focus on justice and peace, it is usually helpful to identify one specific issue and build the service, choice of prayers and hymns around it.

Short readings may be selected from scripture and other appropriate sources.

In the Response section, symbolic action may be employed. It should be clearly explained and offered as an option. People should not feel compelled to participate.

Above all, this service should convey hope for a different future even if it involves lament for what presently has gone wrong.

EXTRA RESOURCES

Opening responses

Leader O God, who called all life into being,
All   **the earth, sea and sky are yours.**

Your presence is all around us;
every atom is full of your energy.

Your Spirit enlivens all who walk the earth.
**With her we yearn for justice to be done,
for creation to be free from threat,
for the hungry to be fed,
for captives to be released,
for your kingdom of peace to come on earth.**

Opening prayer

Leader   O God, gladly we live and move
and have our being in you.
Yet always in the midst of creation's glory,
we see sin's shadow and feel death's darkness.

It is around us in the earth, sea and sky,
   in the abuse of matter.
It is beside us
   in the broken, the hungry and the poor,
   in the betrayal of one another;
   and often, deep within us,
   in a striving against your Spirit.

All   **O Trinity of Love, forgive us
that we may forgive one another,
heal us that we may become people of healing,
and renew us that we may be makers of peace.
Amen.**

Prayer of commitment

Leader   God of new beginnings,
you long for us to live in love and justice
with our neighbours,
with friends and strangers,
with people everywhere.

All	**You call us to be just and loving** **in our working,** **in our shopping,** **in our caring** **and through our prayers.**

Jesus, you were a storyteller,
you talked about money, wages and taxes,
you told stories about integrity and forgiveness,
you helped people who were in trouble,
you listened to people who were sad.
You call us to live as you did –
to listen to each other,
to be forgiving,
and to love our neighbours as we love ourselves.

Holy Spirit, we are discovering what you ask of us.
You are wild and wise and you speak the truth.
You challenge and comfort us,
you breathe life into us,
you shout in the streets and you whisper in our ears.
You remind us what Jesus taught and practised,
you take us to task,
you tell us to turn around;
you call us to walk in Love's way.

Holy Trinity,
God's love in community,
every day
in all our living
help us to say yes to you.
Amen.

Affirmation of faith

Leader   Let us affirm our faith:

All   We believe that God is present
in the darkness before dawn,
in the waiting and uncertainty
where fear and courage join hands,
conflict and caring link arms,
and the sun rises over barbed wire.

We believe in a with-us God
who sits down in our midst to share our humanity.

We affirm a faith that takes us beyond the safe place
into action, into vulnerability,
and into the streets.

We commit ourselves to work for change,
and put ourselves on the line,
to bear responsibility, take risks,
live powerfully and face humiliation;
to stand with those on the edge,
to choose life
and be used by the Spirit
for God's new community of hope.
Amen.

Concluding prayer

Creator of all,
Saviour of all,
Spirit in all,
One God in perfect community,
All   stay with us now.

Where there is apathy,
kindle the flame of your love.

Where there is deceit,
confront every lie with your truth.

Where there is hopelessness,
reveal deep wells of compassion.

Where there is joy,
let your kindly protection be known.

Where we hesitate to serve you,
make us restless until we change.

For yours is the kingdom, the power
and the glory for ever.
Amen

Blessing

Leader   The light of God
to lead us.
The power of God
to hold us.
The joy of God
to heal us.
The grace of God
to caress us.
The love of God
to bless us.
All   **Amen.**

7A Service of Prayers for Healing A

Concerning prayers for healing and the laying on of hands

This service of prayers for healing, which takes place every Tuesday evening, reflects our belief that God's purpose for us all is a life of wholeness, as expressed in the life and teaching of Jesus. The ministry of healing is an integral part of our Christian witness.

We each stand in need of healing, but in this ministry we recognise also the social dimension. The healing of divided communities and nations, and the healing of the earth itself, have their place alongside the healing of broken bodies, hurt minds and wounded hearts, and of the hurts and divisions within ourselves. Our prayers are complementary to the work of medicine and other forms of healing, which are also channels of God's loving and transforming purpose.

In our service we shall name particular people, places and situations for which prayers have been specifically asked. We do this because each person and situation is known to God, not as a problem to be solved, but as a focus for God's acceptance and love. We are not seeking to change God but to change the world; and we trust God that our prayers will be answered, although we do not know when or how healing will happen.

There will also be an opportunity for those who wish to come forward to receive or share in the ministry of the laying on of hands. This can be either for themselves or for another person or situation. In and through this we affirm that the ministry of healing is not restricted to particular individuals but is a corporate, inclusive process – the work of the whole Christian community in which we all have a part to play. God's healing purpose, the promise of God's fulfilling and sustaining love, is for every one of us. Whether we choose to come forward or to remain seated in prayer and concern, God can use our presence in this service.

The Iona Prayer Circle

Iona is the centre of a prayer fellowship of women and men from all over the world committed to praying for people whose names are on our monthly intercessions list. Further information about joining the Prayer Circle, or about having a name added to the monthly list, can be obtained from the Prayer Circle Coordinator at: prayercircle@iona.org.uk

The people gather

Please take time to read the introduction starting on the previous page.

Welcome and introduction

Opening responses

Leader	We gather in your presence, God,
All	**in our need,**
	and bringing with us the needs of the world.

        We come to you, for you come to us in Jesus,
        and you know by experience what human life is like.

        We come with our faith and with our doubts;
        we come with our hopes and with our fears.

        We come as we are, because you have invited us;
        and you have promised never to turn us away.

Song

Prayer

Leader   Loving God,
              you gather us here tonight,

here, where many have come before us
seeking your healing, strength and love.

You know us, God:
you understand who we are,
you know what troubles and puzzles us,
what makes us smile and what makes us sad.
You listen to our questions and our prayers.

You know the people we love, God,
and the people we struggle with.
Sometimes we hurt others;
sometimes we hurt ourselves.

So, we bring our own hurt
asking for your healing;
and we bring the hurt we have caused others
asking for forgiveness.

(a short silence)

Listen to these words of Jesus,
words that we can trust:

'Don't be afraid.'

'I love you.'

'Your sins are forgiven.'

'I will be with you always.'

(pause)

Write these words in our hearts, loving God,
let them take root in our living.

All   **Amen.**

Scripture reading

Short scriptural reflection *(optional)*

Leader	For the word of God in scripture,
	for the word of God among us,
	for the word of God within us,
All	**thanks be to God.**

Prayers for others

Our prayers begin when a basket containing the names of all for whom prayer has been requested in the past week is carried through the church and placed centrally.

After each section of prayer a spoken or sung response is shared. On the occasions when an exceptional number of names is submitted for prayer, we simply share a silence and response at the end of each petition. On these occasions, immediately following the service, people may stay behind, if they wish, to listen and pray as all the names are read aloud.

Invitation to the laying on of hands

As we sing, the leaders will make their way to the prayer circle(s). Those who wish prayer for themselves or others should follow and stand behind one of the kneelers. Any who wish to share in the laying on of hands may also come forward.

When the chant ends, those wishing to receive the ministry kneel or remain standing. A prayer is said by the leader, and then as hands are being laid the congregation may join in the words indicated below in bold.

Chant or song *(standing)*

Prayer of invocation

The laying on of hands *(congregation sits)*

All **Spirit of the living God
present with us now,
heal you in body, mind and spirit
and free you from all that harms you,
in Jesus' name.
Amen.**

When those kneeling have been prayed for, they rise and others take their place. People may resume their seats as and when they wish.

The prayer of St Augustine

Leader Watch now, dear Lord,
with those who wake or watch or weep tonight;
and give your angels charge over those who sleep.

All **Tend your sick ones, O Christ,
rest your weary ones,
bless your dying ones,
soothe your suffering ones,
shield your joyous ones,
and all for your love's sake.**

Song *(optional)*

Blessing

Leader	God to enfold us,
All	**God to surround us.**
	God in our sleeping,
	God in our waking.
	God in our watching,
	God in our hoping.
	God on our lips,
	God in our lives.

(Carmina Gadelica – adapted)

As music plays we leave the church quietly, allowing those who wish to do so to remain in silent prayer. On the occasions when there is an exceptional number of written requests for prayer, all names will be read aloud after those choosing to leave at this point have gone.

Tea and coffee are served in the Refectory, which is through the Residents' door in the cloisters, and left at the top of the stairs.

Please leave quietly.

7B Service of Prayers for Healing B

The people gather

Please take time to read the introduction to this service on pages 109-110.

Welcome and introduction

Opening responses

Leader	Jesus says, 'Ask and you will receive, seek and you will find, knock and the door will be opened.'
All	**Amen.**

        Jesus says, 'Come to me all you who labour
        and are heavy laden.
        I will give you rest.'
        Amen.

        Jesus says, 'Heal the sick.'
        'Feed the hungry.'
        'Free the oppressed.'
        'Watch and pray.'
        Amen.

Song

Prayer

Leader   Eternal God,
             we praise you
             as centuries of people have done
             within these walls.

We are not alone:
saints and angels, invisible, yet in splendour, surround us;
Jesus, the healer, is with us.

Your Holy Spirit leads us to yearn
for our own completeness,
for the well-being of others,
and for a better life.

Fill us with the expectation of goodness;
and should any here feel burdened
by guilt or inadequacy,
let the grace of Jesus
be made real in all its liberating power.

Here let your word come alive in our hearing;
here let our concern respond to your compassion.

Here let hope lead a path through heaviness;
here may your kingdom come.

All **Amen.**

Scripture

Short scriptural reflection *(optional)*

Silence

Prayers for others

Our prayers begin when a basket containing the names of all for whom prayer has been requested in the past week is carried through the church and placed centrally.

After each section of prayer a spoken or sung response is shared. On the occasions when an exceptional number of names is submitted for prayer, we simply share a silence and response at the end of each petition. On these occasions, immediately following the service, people may stay behind, if they wish, to listen and pray as all the names are read aloud.

Invitation to the laying on of hands

As we sing, the leaders will make their way to the prayer circle(s). Those who wish prayer for themselves or others should follow and stand behind one of the kneelers. Any who wish to share in the laying on of hands may also come forward.

When the chant ends, those wishing to receive the ministry kneel or remain standing. A prayer is said by the leader, and then as hands are being laid the congregation may join in the words indicated below in bold.

Chant or song *(standing)*

Prayer of invocation

The laying on of hands *(congregation sits)*

All	**Spirit of the living God** **present with us now,** **heal you in body, mind and spirit** **and free you from all that harms you,** **in Jesus' name.** **Amen.**

When those kneeling have been prayed for, they rise and others take their place. People may resume their seats as and when they wish.

Song *(optional)*

Closing prayer

Leader May the mind of God,
ever wiser than our minds,
search us deeply
and open us to the truths
that make for our healing.

May the ears of God
ever open to our prayers,
listen for us deeply
and hear, beneath our words,
our honest yearnings.

May the heart of God,
ever filled with costly love,
cherish us deeply,
mending any brokenness
and affirming our worth.

All **May God keep us company this night
and bring us joy in the morning.
Amen.**

Adapted from an original prayer by Dorothy McRae McMahon with permission

Blessing

Leader To God be the glory
to the saints and angels be honour,
to those who would work evil be confusion.

To the cross be reverence,
to the church, discernment,
to the departed, new life,

to the penitent, acceptance,
to the suffering, timely healing.

To the four corners of the world be peace,
and on us in this place
may the compassion of God come,
to bless us and overshadow us continually.
Amen.

Ancient Syriac prayer

As music plays we leave the church quietly, allowing those who wish to do so to remain in silent prayer. On the occasions when there is an exceptional number of written requests for prayer, all names will be read aloud after those choosing to leave at this point have gone.

Tea and coffee are served in the Refectory, which is through the Residents' door in the cloisters, and left at the top of the stairs.

Please leave quietly.

7C Appendix to Services of Prayers for Healing

EXTRA RESOURCES

Prayers for others *(1st service)*

Note: Not all the petitions need to be used.

Leader   Jesus,
people came to you when they were in trouble or pain.
Friends carried them,
strangers told you about them;
some invited you into their homes
or met you walking on the road.

You listened to them,
you prayed with them
and you brought hope and healing into their lives.

So tonight we bring into our minds
and hold in God's presence
those for whom we have been asked to pray.

Jesus,
you welcomed children and blessed them;
you gave their parents courage and hope.

So we name before you …
(*names are read, followed by a response or chant*)

    OR

For such as these we pray …
(*short silence, followed by a response or chant*)

Jesus,
through your words and touch
those who were distressed found peace,
and those who were tormented found rest.
So we name before you …

(as above)

Jesus,
you prayed for those who were sick
and you restored them to health.
So we name before you …

(as above)

Jesus,
you wept for the city you loved.
So, we name before you …

(as above)

Jesus,
in your words and actions,
the oppressed found justice
and the angry found release.
So we name before you …

(as above)

Jesus,
you knew the joy of God's presence day by day.
So we name before you …

(as above)

Jesus,
you cried when a friend died,
and you shared the grief of those who mourn.
So we name before you …

(as above)

Jesus,
you taught us to pray.
So, in a moment of silence
we pray for all known to us
who tonight need to know you are near.

(silence)

We thank you,
for all engaged in the ministries of healing
and reconciliation,
for those who work in hospitals and hospices,
for doctors and district nurses,
for carers and counsellors,
for peacemakers and peacekeepers.

God our maker,
Jesus our healer,
Holy Spirit of love and life,
hear our prayers.
To those who seek you,
to all who need you,
to the world you cherish
bring healing,
bring wholeness,
bring peace.

All   **Amen.**

Prayers for others *(2nd service)*

Note: Not all the petitions need to be used.

Leader   Let us pray.
From deep within our being
we call upon you, God,
for through you all can be made whole.

Hear us as we raise to heaven
our concerns for the people of earth.

We pray for those who cry out in physical pain
or who suffer silently
and who long for the healing
that human hands alone cannot offer …

(names read or shared silence, followed by response or chant)

We pray for those who suffer mental anguish,
who worry, feel anxiety, fear the future,
who at night cry, 'I wish to God it were morning,'
and in the morning cry, 'I wish to God it were night' …

(as above)

We pray for those who mourn
who grieve the loss of love or of a loved one,
and for those who know within themselves,
or see in others
a loss of ability or agility
a loss of choice or independence
or a dimming of the light …

(as above)

We pray for those who are near death or fear death,
and for those who have made the last journey
from life to greater life ...

(as above)

And we pray for communities in which people
deal with disaster or terror,
hunger or poverty,
not knowing how or when their misery will end ...

(as above)

In silence we remember
those who are victimised
because of their race, background or history,
because of their gender or sexuality,
because they are different;
and for all who are abused, abandoned or degraded ...

(shared silence followed by response or chant)

And remembering others in our minds,
whose deepest needs may be known to God alone,
we commend them to the affirming and restoring
grace of God.

(shared silence followed by response or chant)

Loving Jesus,
your hands are strong
to hold and heal,
to wipe away tears and protect in danger.
So, hear our prayers.

Protect all those who care for our safety
and bless all those who continue your holy work of healing
in surgeries, hospitals, hospices,
in counselling rooms and around kitchen tables.
We ask these things for the good of your world
and in your strong name.

All **Amen.**

Leader's invitation to laying on of hands

The leader may say these or similar words:

Jesus commanded his disciples to lay hands on and pray for those who needed God's help and healing. This is what we do now.

During the singing, those who wish prayer for themselves or another can make their way to the circle of prayer and stand behind one of the kneelers. When the chant ends, those seeking prayer may kneel or remain standing while those leading lay hands on them using the set prayer in which all may join. When the circle has been completed, others may take a place at the kneelers.

Anyone who wishes to share in the laying on of hands should simply stand behind those seeking prayer and lay a hand or hands on them. Should the group be large, those wishing to share in the ministry should lay a hand on the shoulder of whoever is in front of them. People may join the circle of prayer at any time.

Prayer of invocation *(1st service)*

Leader God our Maker.
You call us to be your presence in the world.
Here, through our hands and prayers,
bring healing, hope and peace.
Amen.

Appendix to Services of Prayers for Healing 127

Prayer of invocation *(2nd service)*

Leader   Come Holy Spirit,
you have placed yearning in our hearts,
now bring healing to body, mind and spirit.
Bless the heads that bow,
the hands that touch,
the hearts that hope.
Bring healing;
bring peace.

Alternative prayer for the laying on of hands

Spirit of the living God
present with us now,
enfold you, body, mind and spirit,
and heal you of all that harms you,
in Jesus' name.
Amen.

Blessing A

Leader   Bless to us O God
the stars that are above us,
the earth that is beneath us,
your image deep within us,
the rest that is before us.
All   **Amen.**

Blessing B

Leader   On our heads and our houses,
All   **the blessing of God.**
In our coming and going,
the peace of God.

In our life and believing,
the love of God.
At our end and new beginning,
the arms of God to welcome us
and bring us home.
Amen.

Suggested chants

Short chants for use as prayer responses:

> Kyrie (Ghana, Ukraine or Iona)
> Lord, draw near (Iona)
> Lord Jesus Christ, lover of all (Iona)

Longer chants for use as people move for the laying on of hands:

> Come, bring your burdens to God (South Africa)
> Come to me (Iona)
> Don't be afraid (Iona)
> Lord of Life, we come to you (Scotland)
> Ubi caritas et amor – Where there is love and caring, God is there – (Taizé)

Note on winter variation:

In winter, services are held in the more intimate and marginally warmer Michael Chapel. The Service of Prayers for Healing has been adapted to make best use of the space and size of the group gathered for worship. Instead of people coming forward for the laying on of hands, a lighted candle is passed from one person to the next around the chapel. Those wishing prayer will continue to hold it, and during this pause the congregation will say together the prayer 'Spirit of the Living God ...'

All year round, large numbers of people send requests for prayers for healing. This weekly service includes their requests.

8A An Act of Commitment A

We are here because Jesus calls us. Jesus is not neutral about those he loves. He does not want them simply to bask in his generosity, but to discover depths and potentials within themselves that are only found through commitment.

Jesus calls us to be committed to his person, because it was to relate personally to humanity that he came. But he also invites us to be committed to a style of life which represents on earth the qualities of heaven.

And Jesus calls us to a purpose: the redemption of all things – social, political, personal and religious – in accordance with the revealed will of God.

In this service, we are given the opportunity to recommit ourselves to Jesus and the purposes of God's kingdom. This may happen in a variety of ways, some of which may involve moving within the church. Such active engagement enables prayer in ways different from simply using words; however, it is always optional, and to remain seated and make a personal commitment is equally appropriate.

The people gather

Welcome and introduction

Opening responses

Leader	To Pharisees minding their business, and fishermen mending their nets:
All	**'Follow me!'**
	To the money-handlers, the lawyers, the intellectuals, the power-brokers:
	'Follow me!'

To the carers and the cleaners,
the married, the single,
the young and the old,
country-folk and city-dwellers:
'Follow me!'

Then and now,
together and apart,
willing or doubting,
ready or not,
Jesus says:
'Follow me!'

Song

Prayer of approach

Word *(may be followed by a brief reflection)*

Invitation to commitment

Song or chant

Making a sign of commitment

Affirmation

All   We believe and trust in God
who has created and is creating,
who has come in Jesus –
the Word made flesh –
to reconcile and make new,

and who works in us and others
by the power of the Spirit.

We are called to be the church:
to celebrate God's presence,
to live with respect for creation,
to love and serve others,
to seek justice and resist evil,
to proclaim Jesus, crucified and risen,
our judge and hope.

In life and death,
in life beyond death,
God is with us.
We are not alone.
Thanks be to God.
Amen.[1]

Prayer of commitment

Leader   In gratitude for this moment,
this place,
those around us,
Christ among us,
we give ourselves
to you our God.

Take us out to live as changed people
because we have met the risen Christ
and cannot be the same.

All   Ask much of us,
expect much from us.
enable much by us,
encourage many through us.

So may we live to your glory
both as inhabitants of earth
and citizens of the commonwealth of heaven.
Amen.

Closing song

Blessing

Leader   Now may God,
who gives seed to the sower
and grain to the reaper,
provide all that we need
so that we may produce a rich harvest
of faith, love, justice and joy
for the good of the earth and its people
and to the glory of God.
Amen.

---

[1] A New Creed from *Voices United: The Hymn and Worship Book of The United Church of Canada*. United Church Publishing House, 1996, p. 918. Used with permission. For the current version, see page 146.

8B An Act of Commitment B

The people gather

Please read the notes regarding this service at the beginning of the previous liturgy on page 129.

Welcome and introduction

Opening responses

Leader God has told us what is good;
All God has told us what is right.
We are to live justly:
we are to live justly.
We are to love kindly:
we are to love kindly.
We are to walk humbly:
we are to walk with God.

Song

Prayer of approach

Leader You call us, God.
You call us to walk in your way.
You show us in Jesus how we should live.
You give us your Holy Spirit to keep us right.
And we are grateful.

Love and justice are what you require of us, God –
love for you and love and justice for ourselves
and our neighbours.

And we try.
And sometimes we get it right
and sometimes we fail,
but we try.

(a silence)

Thank you for these words of Jesus
which summon us and give us life:

Don't be afraid.
You are forgiven.
I call you friends.
Come and follow me.

All **Amen.**

Word *(may be followed by a brief reflection)*

Affirmation of faith

Leader   Let us affirm our faith:

All   **We believe in God
who made the sea and the earth, the sun and the sky,
who calls us to live responsibly.**

**We believe in Jesus Christ
who became human,
who healed the sick,
who talked to children,
who made friends with sinners.
He burned brightly and offended many.
His journey was one of life and death and resurrection.
His light continues to shine in the darkness.**

We believe in the Holy Spirit
who inspired the scriptures,
and whose breath we breathe.

We believe that God calls us to be a community,
committed to one another,
offering a welcome to everyone,
old and young, rich and poor,
strong and weak.

We believe that God calls us to be peacemakers,
workers for justice,
brothers and sisters,
a light for our world. Amen.

(written by two fourteen-year-old boys in a workshop on Iona)

Invitation to commitment

Song or chant

Act of commitment

Leader   I invite you, wherever you are in the church, to join in the prayer of commitment.

We say together:

All   Loving God,
you call me.
In the presence of your people
I make you this promise –
I will follow Jesus,
I will walk with you. Amen.

Song

Sending

Leader: God has told us what is good;
All **God has told us what is right.**

Do you believe that the Gospel commands us to seek peace founded on justice?
We do.

Then, will you live justly?
We will live justly.

Will you love kindly?
We will love kindly.

Will you walk with God?
We will walk with God.

Blessing

The blessing of God
sure, strong and kindly
be around us
and within us
now
and all the nights and days
of our journey home.

All **Amen.**

8C Appendix to Acts of Commitment

Notes on the act of commitment

This is not a second Justice and Peace service in which we intercede for the world and its people, but rather a time when we seriously ally ourselves to following Jesus.

There are two basic ways in which people can actively participate in an act of commitment.

Symbolic action around the church (8A)

This involves a time when people may move from their seats and make a sign of their commitment to Jesus and/or the purposes of God's kingdom. For example, people may move to one of several stations around the church to light a candle, write something, place a symbol, receive something. These prayerful actions should embody the person's desire to make a sign of their commitment.

The leader should choose a passage of scripture which illustrates or encourages commitment, then clearly indicate what is going to happen. During symbolic action, music sung or played will enable some to move and all to participate.

Coming forward to receive words of Jesus (8B)

This is the original way the Iona Community held this service in the Abbey. It requires kneelers to be laid out, appropriately spaced, in front of the communion table.

The leader should choose a portion of scripture which deals specifically with discipleship, the decision to follow Jesus. After reading the text, the leader may make some brief comments on how Jesus calls us to a personal, not a theoretical, relationship, and for some people this might be the time to make or remake a commitment to him. People are invited to follow the leader down to the communion table where they will individually be reminded of some words of Jesus.

RESOURCES FOR THE SERVICE

Prayer of approach (a)

Leader   God, our Creator,
you have wonderfully made us.

You have planted in us different gifts,
no two of us are the same.
On our own we may or may not shine,
but together, in your company,
you turn us into a kaleidoscope of grace.

Sometimes we lament the busyness of our lives,
sometimes we bemoan the emptiness.
These are signs of our longing
for a fulfilment we cannot create,
but which we can receive
from the One who made, knows and loves us.

Lover of all and of each,
enable us here to be fully open
to you
to all you have to offer,
to all that you ask of us.
Amen.

Prayer of approach (b)

Leader Eternal God,
in this old and sacred space
for generation after generation
Jesus has surprised people, challenged presumptions,
embraced, inspired and encouraged.

We are here not to worship the past
and celebrate its dead heroes;
we are here to anticipate your future.
We are here not to remember the good we have done,
but to prepare for what we might yet do
by making room for the Holy Spirit
to reshape us.

So, make this time and this space
a holy gathering,
an arena of grace,
a touching place
where Christ can gather us for God.

In his name we pray.
Amen

Words of scripture

A biblical passage which reflects the call of God may be opened up through reading, drama, reflection or conversation or use of other media.

Invitation to commitment

Service 8A
The leader should explain how the congregation may participate in the symbolic action to make a sign of their commitment. The words should be simple and clear and always presented as an invitation – giving the option to participate but also to choose to remain seated and continue in prayer. The action may naturally begin as the congregation begins to sing the chant which follows the invitation.

Service 8B – the following or similar words may be said:

> Jesus invites us to follow him,
> to make new beginnings in our lives.
>
> Now is an opportunity to do that.
>
> At the end of the next song, as music continues to play (*or if an easily remembered chant is being sung:* As we begin to sing the chant), those who want to personally commit or recommit themselves to Jesus may follow me to the front of the church and stand behind one of the kneelers. Please bring the worship book with you. After sharing a prayer of commitment together, those who remain in the seats will sit while those at the front kneel and are reminded individually of the words of Jesus.
>
> We now sing …
> and if you are coming to the front, please remember to bring your worship book.

As music continues to play at the end of the song, or during the chant, the leader walks to the front of the church and stands in front of the communion table facing the congregation. S/he invites people to turn to page 135 for the prayer of commitment.

At its conclusion the congregation is invited to sit and those standing at the front to kneel. The leader then goes round those who are kneeling and, laying a hand or hands on people's shoulders, reminds them of the words of Jesus, as are listed on page 144 thus:

> Jesus says,
> 'I call you my friend.'
>
> Jesus says,
> 'Do not be afraid'
>
> etc.

At the end of this action, people return to their seats as the previous song or chant is hummed, or as music plays.

Affirmation of faith (a)

Leader   God said, 'Let there be light.'

All   We believe in a bright and amazing God,
who has been to the depths of despair
on our behalf;
who has risen in splendour and majesty;
who decorates the universe
with sparkling water, clear white light,
twinkling stars and sharp colours,
over and over again.

We believe that Jesus is the light of the world;
that God believes in us, forgives and trusts us,
even though we make the same mistakes
over and over again.

We commit ourselves
to Jesus,

and so to one another as sisters and brothers,
renewing our life as a human family
over and over again.
We commit ourselves
to asking questions
to being open to illumination
to living in the light of the Spirit.
Amen.

Affirmation of faith (b)

Leader	We believe in God
All	**who is older than eternity**

**and younger than our next breath;
who is beyond describing
yet knows us all by name;
who inspires faith
yet cannot be contained by religion.**

We believe in Jesus Christ,
flesh of our flesh, bone of our bone;
**he came in the body
to give worth to every human life.
He touched the untouchable,
loved the unlovable
and endured slander, persecution and death.**

We believe that God's Kingdom comes on earth
through Christ's suffering love.
**He rose from the grave as living proof
that what is laid down in faith
will be raised in glory.
He ascended to heaven
to be present at all times to all people.**

We believe in the Holy Spirit,
who leads us into truth and freedom,
who gives good gifts to all God's children,
who works through prayer and politics,
through justice, care of creation
and the healing of the nations.

We celebrate the potential God has given:
the life in our bodies,
the yearning in our souls,
the promise of good things in store
for those who love and serve their maker.

Prayer of commitment

Leader Into your hands we commit ourselves, O Christ,
for your holding,
your directing,
your inspiring,
your perfecting.

Into your hands we commit ourselves.

All Bless us with your power
to heal, help, liberate and challenge.
Bless us with your yearning
for a better world and a fuller faith.
Bless us with your Holy Spirit
within us and among us.
Amen.

List of words of Jesus

Jesus says:

I call you my friend.
Do not be afraid.
You are the salt of the earth.
I am the vine, you are the branch.
What you do to the least of people, you do to me.
Give to others and God will give to you.
Let your light shine before other people.
The hairs of your head have been counted.
Seek and you will find.
Love each other as I have loved you.
The truth will make you free.
You will shine like the sun in the kingdom of heaven.
I am the good shepherd. My sheep know my voice.
Turn around and believe the good news.
Come to me, you who are weary; I will give you rest.
I am the good shepherd. No one can take my sheep away from me.
Don't store up riches for yourself on earth.
Whoever welcomes a child in my name welcomes me.
You did not choose me. I chose you.
Love your enemies and do good to them.
Do not worry about tomorrow; each day has enough troubles of its own.
Love God with your heart, mind and strength and love your neighbour as yourself.
Those who work for peace are called children of God.
I love you as God loves me.
I will send the Holy Spirit to help you.
I have come that you might have life in its fullness.
Let my joy be in you so that your joy will be complete.
You are light for the world.
Never mind what others do; I want you to follow me.

Closing responses

Leader	The cross …
All	**we shall take it.**

The bread …
we shall break it.

The pain …
we shall bear it.

The joy …
we shall share it.

The gospel …
we shall live it.

The love …
we shall give it.

The light …
we shall cherish it.

The darkness …
God shall perish it.

Current version of the affirmation on pp130-131:

We are not alone,
  we live in God's world.

We believe in God:
  who has created and is creating,
  who has come in Jesus,
    the Word made flesh,
    to reconcile and make new,
  who works in us and others
    by the Spirit.

We trust in God.

We are called to be the Church:
  to celebrate God's presence,
  to live with respect in Creation,
  to love and serve others,
  to seek justice and resist evil,
  to proclaim Jesus, crucified and risen,
    our judge and our hope.

In life, in death, in life beyond death,
  God is with us.
We are not alone.

  Thanks be to God.

A New Creed from *Voices United: The Hymn and Worship Book of The United Church of Canada*. United Church Publishing House, 1996, p. 918. Used with permission.

9A Ceilidh Communion

The people gather

The Thursday evening service of Holy Communion is very different from the Sunday morning one. We are not gathered facing the altar, but rather sit around a table or tables.

Jesus was often found at meals; the Gospels record over twenty instances. It was there he deepened friendships, heard stories and challenged assumptions in the giving and receiving of hospitality.

In the context of this table companionship, the Last Supper was celebrated. And it is this sense of hospitable community that we draw on this evening, as well as the Scottish ceilidh tradition of sharing music, story and song.

As you gather, please feel free to speak to those around you, allowing this ancient place of prayer to be also a place of everyday welcome.

Welcome and introduction

Responses

Leader   For the joy of human company,
shared stories, friendly laughter
and conversations that change us,
All   **thanks be to God.**

For a place that spans the ages
and is home to all who gather,
thanks be to God.

For the wonder of life,
and the decision of God to come among us,
thanks be to God.

How can we keep from singing?
Nothing can keep us from singing.

Song

The story sequence

A story from this week
... followed by a conversation and a short song to finish.

A story from the Bible *(see options in appendix)*
... followed by a conversation and a short song to finish.

The Story of the Table
... leading into the celebration of Holy Communion.

Invitation

Prayer

Celebrant   Let us pray.

We love you, Holy God.

We love you for the feast that is life:
friendships and laughter,
intimacy and trust,
moments of discovering deep truth,
hidden potentials we never knew we had,
and beauty –
serene beauty and rugged beauty,
the world you have crafted
and the words, the sounds, the colours
with which people reflect and explore life.

All	**We love you, holy God**
for not leaving us alone,
because in Jesus you became tangible:
hands touched him,
tears touched him,
generosity touched him.

And he has touched us.
That is why we are here.
That is why across time and eternity
we sing (say) because we cannot keep silent:

Holy, holy, holy
God of power and might,
heaven and earth are full of your glory.
Hosanna in the highest.

Blessed is the one who comes
in the name of our God.
Hosanna in the highest.

God, we have been gathered by you,
caught in your net,
summoned to your table.

As we open ourselves to your generous hospitality,
let your Spirit move among us
and be present in the food we share
so that this bread and wine become for us
the living presence of Jesus.

Open our eyes to see him,
our ears to hear him,
our hands to hold him,
our hearts to receive him,
our souls to cherish him.
Amen. |

The Sharing

Celebrant   As Jesus broke bread,
             we break this bread.

             (bread is broken)

             As Jesus took wine
             we take this cup.

             (cup is lifted)

             As his first disciples shared communion
             in an upstairs room,
             we share these gifts from hand to hand,
             and feed on them in our hearts
             with love and gratitude.

The bread is broken and, with the wine, is shared for all. We pass it to each other in respectful silence. If, for any reason, you do not wish to receive the bread or the wine, simply take it from the person who offers it and pass it to the person beside you.

The peace

We share a sign of Christ's peace with each other.

Closing song(s)

Closing responses

Leader	Is God good?
All	**God is good.**

        Is life worth living?
        Life is worth living.

        Is the best yet to come?
        Always, the best is yet to come.

        Then go,
        as friends of Jesus
        and enjoy him for ever.
        Amen.

9B A Ceilidh Service

The people gather

This service is based on the Gaelic tradition of ceilidhs (pronounced kaylies), informal gatherings in people's homes presided over by a Fear-an-taigh or Bean-an-taigh (man or woman of the house). They would be an opportunity to share music and stories, and maybe food and drink. There might also be dancing. The emphasis would be on simple hospitality (fàilte, pronounced fel-che, meaning welcome), enjoyment of community and shared skills. The sharing of food in this service is similar to an agapé – a reminder of the ministry of the whole people of God. People are invited to greet those around them briefly and to learn the name of at least one new person.

Welcome and introduction

Opening words *(other choices in the appendix)*

Leader	Fàilte – you're all welcome
Voice A	Welcome, worshippers, making room for all who come;
B	welcome, neighbours, cooried in together, keeping warm;
C	welcome, colleagues, with whom we work each day;
D	welcome, friends we've made along the way;
A	welcome, companions with whom we've sat at table;
B	welcome, former strangers, now we know your names;
C	welcome to this time we'll spend with each other;
D	welcome, with the different gifts we bring together.
Leader	Be sure that God welcomes all that we can offer, and lovingly invites each one of us to this celebration. Fàilte!
All	**Thank you, God. Amen.**

Songs and setting of the table

As we sing, the table or tables are made ready.

The story sequence

Prayer

Leader   God, who created this blue-green planet,
blessed with water –
springs, burns and rivers
flowing down to the great ocean,
mist and rain helping the land grow green –
we thank you for water, reflecting light, giving life.

God, who clothes the machair
with flowers of every colour and fragrance,
who gives the birds of the air berries and grain and grubs,
we thank you that we have food today
and faith in tomorrow.

All   **Whenever we taste food or water
may we remember those who hunger and thirst;
and, as we are nourished, may we gain energy
to work for a greater sharing in your world.
Amen.**

Pouring and sharing

Leader   As we pour out clean, cool water – which is present on the table at every meal we share, and is carried on pilgrimage to quench our thirst – we remember the Living Water with which God surprises us and enriches and transforms our lives.

The water is poured out and remains on the table as a symbol.

Other symbolic actions may vary with each service, and may engage one or more of the five senses. Passing things round, looking, listening, smelling, tasting will be accompanied by words such as these:

Leader   As we share and hold these simple things, we thank God for all that gives life meaning ... for our daily bread, for food that nourishes and delights us ... and for companionship and laughter that sustain us ...

And we share silence, too.

Sharing silence

Chant or other music

Closing responses

Leader   Go with joy:
may you be surprised by angels
and join in their laughter.

Group A   Go with empty hands:
may you receive the generosity of others
and the blessings of God.

Group B   Go with full hearts:
may you find opportunities
to share all you have been given.

Leader	Go in the love of the Maker: who gives us life and calls us by name.
Group A	Go in the love of the Son: who walks with us.
Group B	Go in the love of the Spirit: who feeds us and leads us home.
Leader	Go in peace.
All	**Go in peace.**

Blessing

Leader	God bless each of us as we travel on: may we discover tables spread in the wilderness and companions on the road.
All	**Amen**

Song or chant *(as recessional)*

9C Appendix to the Ceilidh and Ceilidh Communion Services

NOTES FOR THE CEILIDH *COMMUNION*

The story sequence

The first story has to be arranged in advance. It should come from a guest or a member of staff who, during the week, has made a discovery or shared an insight which it would be good for all to hear, and who feels comfortable about sharing it. It is followed by a conversation in which people are asked to turn to each other and either reflect on what has been said or tell each other a story of their own from the week.

The second story comes from the Bible. It should be briefly put into context, read clearly and be followed by another question to enable conversation. Such questions might be:

a) Which person in that story do you most identify with and why?
b) If you could ask one question of one character in the story, who would that be and what would you ask?

With regard to the second story, it might be best (if the text is short) to have it read, then ask the question and have it read again. This is particularly important if it cannot be guaranteed that everyone is familiar with the biblical passage **or** if there are people in the congregation for whom English is not their first language.

There is no 'feedback' after these conversations, but the same chant, taught in advance, should end the opening and story conversations.

The third story (the story of the table) is that of the institution of Holy Communion. It can be read from 1st Corinthians 11:23-26 or from the text in the **EXTRA RESOURCES** section below.

EXTRA RESOURCES FOR CEILIDH *COMMUNION*

Bible stories suitable for discussion

Abraham and the angels	Genesis 18:1-15
Manna in the wilderness	Exodus 16:9-15
Elijah and the ravens	1 Kings 17:1-6
Elijah and the widow	1 Kings 17:7-16
Jesus and Matthew	Matthew 9:9-15
Jesus and Zaccheus	Luke 19:1-10
The wedding feast	John 2:1-10
Lazarus's house	John 12:1-8
Jairus	Luke 8:40-42 & 49-56
Syro-Phoenician woman	Mark 7:24-30
Simon the leper	Matthew 26:6-13
Simon the Pharisee	Luke 7:36-50
Feeding of the 5000	John 6:1-15
Parable of the great feast	Luke 14:16-24
Dives and Lazarus	Luke 16:19-31

Post-resurrection meals:

Emmaus road	Luke 24:13-35
Upstairs room	Luke 24:36-49
Lakeside barbecue	John 21:1-14

Story of the table

Reader   It was on a night when old, familiar stories were retold that Jesus and his friends engaged in the sacred meal which Jews call the Passover.

During that meal, rich in food and memory,
Jesus took a piece of bread.
And after he had blessed it,
he broke it and said,

'This is my body. It is given for you.
Do this to remember me.'

Later in the meal, he took a cup of wine,
and having given thanks over it,
he gave it to his disciples with the words,
'In this cup is the new relationship with God
made possible because of my death.
Drink it, all of you, to remember me.'

Invitation *(these or other words)*

Celebrant   Gathered round this table,
we will do what Jesus did,
and what he asked his disciples to do
throughout the ages.

We are all invited to share in this meal,
whether we regularly receive communion,
whether we have never been at such a celebration,
or whether indeed we have given up on God.

At this table, it is neither our virtues nor our defects
that are important.
It is the invitation to each and to all
to take what Jesus has to offer those
with whom he is pleased to dine.

NOTES FOR THE CEILIDH *SERVICE*

Set up and introduction

The congregation gathers to sit either round a long table between the choir stalls, or in the nave, in clusters of chairs, with small tables if possible. As people gather there is instrumental music to create a relaxed and welcoming atmosphere.

There is an initial welcome and an introduction to the shape of the service together with any brief necessary announcements. The leader can explain that they are taking a key role in traditional ceilidhs: the Bean-an-taigh (Ben an tie) or Fear-an-taigh (Feer an tie) – the woman or man of the house in Gaelic – is there to make sure that everyone feels welcome (explain that is what fàilte (fel-che) means).

Then, in an activity that mirrors the Saturday evening service, participants are invited to greet the person next to or opposite them by name – or to learn their name. Ideally this will include everyone, including those who have only just arrived on the island.

The setting of the table

Possibly three songs are sung together, none too long, e.g. global church songs/chants. This could include learning one which will be reprised later in the service. In between the songs, short informal links will make sense of the selection and give time for change of instruments etc.

During the singing, things may be brought to the table(s) and passed down its length (e.g. oatcakes, bowls of shells or seeds, craftwork from the week, water poured into jugs).

The story sequence: two stories, a conversation and a song

1st story

Someone who has been identified during the week tells a story, or gives a testimony, no longer than five minutes, to do with food or meals. It should enable others to tell their own stories later, in response to a question.

Optional song or chant

2nd story

A passage from the Bible involving a meal is told as a story, rather than read from the lectern. Possible stories are listed in the extra resources section.

Conversation

A question is asked, music is played while we consider it, and then we share our reflections with people around us. The conversation will be brought to a close when we reprise a song already sung:

Song

Possible questions which may naturally arise from the stories

a) When did you most enjoy a meal with strangers?
b) What is the most exotic food you've ever shared?
c) When were you at a meal when someone said something which embarrassed the host or the guests?
d) When in your experience was a meal made out of a morsel?
e) Which meal did you enjoy most this week? Why?
f) 'Companions' are those with whom we share bread. When has this come home to you?

EXTRA RESOURCES FOR CEILIDH *SERVICE*

Opening words (a)

Leader   Creator of community,
All   **we gather in your name.**
            Generous and inclusive Friend,
            we rejoice in our friendship here.
            Lover of laughter and song,
            we offer these to you.
            Giver of our daily bread,
            we thank you for all that nourishes us.
            God, our constant Companion,
            be present in all our sharing.

Opening words (b)

Words which mean 'welcome' in as many languages as possible are called out from around the church – these may be scripted and prepared or invited and spontaneous. Where possible a roving microphone should be used. This interlude is brought to a close by:

Leader: Be sure that God welcomes all that we can offer,
             and lovingly welcomes each one of us tonight.
All   **Thank you, God. Amen**

Bible stories *(see above)*

Suggested chants

Quiet/reflective
South African Alleluia
God, fill our lives to overflowing

Jesus Christ, Jesus Christ, Son of God among us
The peace of the earth
Ubi caritas

Recessional
Mayenziwe
South African Amen
Celtic Amen
Duncan Alleluia
Halle halle halle
Ameni
Amen siyakudumisa
We will walk with God

Blessing (a)

Leader	Giving God, bless all who have gathered round this table. May we know the fullness of your presence at every meal and in all our sharing.
All	**Amen**

Blessing (b)

Leader	Generous God, in our world some hunger for food, and others for meaning; you have blessed this place and time, where we have been fed in many ways; bless us now, as we go on – sharing food for the journey, finding companions on the way.
All	**Amen**

10A Creation Liturgy

The people gather

God calls humanity to care for Creation. Throughout the ages, the Christian church has not always paid due attention to this divine expectation. But in recent years, with the threat and experience of climate change, we cannot, in prayer or action, be neutral.

Welcome and introduction

Opening responses

Leader 1   God above us –
           trees, birds and sunshine,
           stars and moonlight –
All   **God above us.**

Leader 2   God beneath us –
           earth, rocks and rivers,
           roots and caverns –
           God beneath us.

Leader 3   God around us –
           seas, winds and cities,
           animals and people –
           God around us.

Leader 4   God within us –
           hope, tears and laughter,
           love and wonder –
           God within us.

Leader 5	God above us, God beneath us, God around us, God within us,
All	**we celebrate that you made us, you love us and you call us to work and rest with you.**

Song

Prayer of thanks for creation

Leader	Let us pray.

Thank you, God,
thanks for beauty:
the twinkle in an older person's eye,
a child's shout of laughter;
thanks for greening trees and frozen waterfalls,
stunning buildings and flowerbeds in summer.

All **Thanks for beauty.**

Thank you, God,
thanks for creativity:
the skills of a tapestry weaver,
the imagination of a web designer;
thanks for bakers and dancers and crossword compilers,
for spiders' webs and city murals.
Thanks for creativity.

Thank you, God,
thanks for abundance:
for seeds and raindrops,
for grains of sand and infinite galaxies;

thanks for seagulls, plankton and shoals of mackerel,
for wriggling worms and golden dandelions.
Thanks for abundance.

Thanks for your world, God,
and for our part in it.
Thanks that you are a maker,
and that you made us makers too.

Help us to love creation as you love it,
to take risks to value it as Jesus did,
and draw us into the wildness and wonder
of your Holy Spirit
today and every day.
Amen.

Readings

Prayer of regret

Leader   In the light of your word
and your call to care for creation,
we come to say sorry, God.

We're sorry for the times we've messed up,
sorry for bad decisions we've made,
sorry for people we've hurt,
sorry for damaging your world.

In the silence, we seek your forgiveness for ourselves
and healing for the world.

(moment of quiet)

Listen to what God says to us:
'I made the heavens and the earth.

| | I call you to be good servants and responsible stewards.
Come and work with me.
I will always be with you.' |
|-------|---|
| **All** | **Amen.** |

Reflection

Which may include drama, symbolic action, testimony, conversation or some other media.

Song

Closing blessing

Leader	May the heavens bless you.
May the sun shine on you.
May the rain dance on your wellies.
May the stars make you wonder and smile.
	May the earth bless you,
and may you bless the earth
in planting and protest,
and sharing food.
All	**Amen.**

Closing responses

Leader	Go now
Voice 1	Go and revel in God's world
Voice 2	Go and be creative
Voice 3	Go and work for justice
Voice 4	Go and love your neighbours
Voice 5	Go and walk with God.
All	**Amen.**

10B Appendix to Creation Liturgy

Opening responses

Leader In the corncrake's rasp and the skylark's song:
All   God's joy at the heart of all things

In the gap-toothed grin of a mischievous child:
God's joy at the heart of all things

In the tantalising smell of freshly baked bread:
God's joy at the heart of all things

In the starlit splendour of the winter sky:
God's joy at the heart of all things

In the satisfying squelch of a muddy walk:
God's joy at the heart of all things

In the ladybird's flight and the puffin's waddle:
God's joy at the heart of all things

In the sharing of stories and sipping of beer:
God's joy at the heart of all things

In the windswept hair of a highland cow:
God's joy at the heart of all things

When children are able to be children:
God's joy at the heart of all things

When adults become like children again:
God's joy at the heart of all things

(Written on Iona with guests)

Blessing

Leader May God the Creator who made heaven and earth
bless us with creativity and wonder.

May Jesus who walked through fields and cities
bless us with kind hands and listening ears.

May the Holy Spirit who is around us and within us
bless us with the courage to be caring and just.

All **May we work and walk
in the strong love of the Trinity
all our nights and days.
Amen.**

SUGGESTED READINGS

From scripture

Genesis	1:1-2,4
Psalms	19:1-6
	29:1-11
	65:6-13
	84:1-12
	96:1-13
	97:1-12
	104:1-35
	147:1-20
	148:1-14
Proverbs	8:12 & 22-31
Job	Ch. 38 & 39
Ecclesiasticus (Sirach)	42:15-26; 43:1-28
Isaiah	40:21-31

Matthew	6:24-34
John	1:1-4
Colossians	1:15-20

Words for readings and reflection from other sources

FROM A SPEECH BY CHIEF SEATTLE IN 1854:

Leader   This we know, the earth does not belong to us:
All   **we belong to the earth.**

This we know, all things are connected:
like the blood which unites one family.

For we did not weave the web of life:
we are merely a strand of it.

Whatever we do to the web,
we do to ourselves.

ALFIE SANG (*from Save the Children*)

Alfie was small, fat and three years old. Too small to go to school, too big to be kept safely in a pram. The flat Alfie lived in was small; on the 18th floor of a huge block of flats. He could only come down when his mother went shopping. And then there were only lift shafts, stone stairs, crowded streets, and if the lift was out of order there were 200 steps to climb.

Alfie liked noise – the shouting, stamping, banging kind. But the lady in the flat below did not like people stamping on her ceiling, and the man next door did not like shouting. Alfie liked sand and water. But sand scratched the floors and water made a mess. Sometimes Alfie cried.

One day Alfie's mother took him downstairs; not to go shopping, but to a hall near the flats. There were children everywhere. Sitting at tables, climbing up ladders, shouting, laughing, banging. There were swings and see-saws, blocks and tins, books and papers. Alfie did not know where to begin.

That afternoon, all the way back to the little flat on the 18th floor, Alfie sang. All his mother heard was a solemn, tuneless chant, but actually Alfie was singing of the glory of noise, of the stamping of feet, the banging of hammers, the shouting out loud. He sang of climbing and running and rolling; of the roughness of sand, the wetness of water and the rainbow beauty of paints, and of the pleasures of friends; and he sang because he knew he could go again the next day.

From the mystics

A. FROM MEDITATIONS WITH HILDEGARD OF BINGEN

> The earth is at the same time mother.
> She is mother of all that is natural,
> mother of all that is human.

> She is mother of all,
> for contained in her are the seeds of all.

> The earth of humankind contains all moistness,
> all verdancy,
> all germinating power.

> It is in so many ways fruitful.

> All creation comes from it,
> yet it forms not only the basic raw material for humankind
> but also the substance of the incarnation of God's Son.

B. FROM MEDITATIONS WITH JULIAN OF NORWICH

I saw that God was everything that is good
and encouraging.

God is our clothing
that wraps, clasps and encloses us
so as never to leave us.

God showed me in my palm
a little thing round as a ball
about the size of a hazelnut.

I looked at it with the eye of my understanding
and asked myself:
'What is this thing?'
And I was answered: 'It is everything that is created.'

I wondered how it could survive since it seemed so little
it could suddenly disintegrate into nothing.

The answer came: 'It endures and ever will endure,
because God loves it.'

And so everything has being because of God's love.

C. FROM MEDITATIONS WITH MEISTER ECKHART

Apprehend God in all things,
for God is in all things.

Every single creature is full of God
and is a book about God.
Every creature is a word of God.

If I spent enough time with the tiniest creature –
even a caterpillar –
I would never have to prepare a sermon.
So full of God
is every creature.

11A Evening Liturgy

The people gather

Welcome and introduction

Opening responses

Leader This is the time
when light fades
and shadows lengthen
and sounds are subdued –
all as God intended.
All **Amen.**

This is the time
when bodies relax,
minds unwind,
and tiredness comes –
all as God intended.
Amen

This is the time
when others greet the morning
while we meet the night,
and the world continues to sing,
in all the accents of creation,
a love-song to its Maker.
Blessed be God's Name.

Song

Prayer

Leader   Come, brother Jesus, be our guest,
stay with us for day is ending.

Bring to this place your poverty,
All   **for then shall we be rich.**
Bring to this place your pain,
that in sharing it, we may also share your joy.
Bring to this place your understanding of us,
that we may be freed to learn more of you.
Bring to this place your Holy Spirit,
that we and all things might be made new.

With friend, with stranger,
with the unknown and well known ones
be among us tonight,
for the doors of this house are open,
and the doors of our hearts we leave ajar.

Scripture

Leader   In the world many things happen at night:
people travel, people meet,
people have secret conversations,
people lie awake restless,
people sleep through exhaustion.

And this has always been so;
holy books bear witness to it.
So let us hear a night story from the Bible.

A story is read and may be followed by conversation or silence.

Night prayer

Leader What if the darkness covers us
and the day around us turns to night?
Darkness is not too dark for God
to whom dark and light are one.

Let us pray

You never sleep, God.
You are always awake, always watching,
always willing the world and its people
to turn in the right direction.

So tonight, will you comfort those who cannot sleep
because of illness,
or worry,
or fear;
or for reasons they cannot understand.

(pause)

God be near them.
All **God be near them.**

And tonight will you be close to those who wait
patiently or impatiently
for a birth
or a death,
for a visit,
or for the pieces of their life's jigsaw to fit together.

(pause)

God be near them.
God be near them.

And tonight will you be close to those who wonder,
who look for inspiration,
who long to be with the one or the ones they love,
who hope to recognise the right time
when they can say 'I'm sorry,'
or 'I love you,'
or even 'Enough is enough.'

(pause)

God be near them.
God be near them.

And God, listen to us
as we share with you
whatever joys or sorrows,
discoveries or questions
we will take with us into the night.

(pause)

God be near us,
God be near us.

Into your hands we commit ourselves –
our souls, our bodies, our minds, our futures –
for all things come from you
and are best kept in your care.
Amen

Evening song

Closing responses

Leader   For the day now done
All   **thanks be to God.**

              For the rest before us
              thanks be to God.

              Because God never sleeps
              so that we can,
              thanks be to God.

              But before the day is done,
              let God's holy name be praised;
              and let God's people say Amen.
              Amen.

11B Appendix to Evening Liturgy

NOTES FOR THE SERVICE

This service may be led in a lit environment, with the congregation engaging in printed responses. Or it may be led with leaders only having access to the text, in which case they read words in bold as well as standard type.

Scripture

Below is listed a variety of stories which relate to the night. Not all are stories of piety or peace. Some are quite gruelling, but bad things sometimes happen at night. The story (which may well be unknown) should be read calmly like a bedtime story, irrespective of the content.

The reading may be followed by a silence for reflection. Or there might be a conversation between people sitting close to each other and with no need for feedback at its conclusion. To facilitate this, the leader could pose a question such as:

a) Why do you think that of all God could inspire to be included in the Bible, this story has been included?

b) What is the main question that comes to your mind when you hear this story?

c) If there were a sequel to this story, what would you hope it contained?

d) If you were to paint an abstract picture inspired by this story, which colours would you choose and why?

Before giving time for conversation, it might be helpful to have the passage read a second time, by a different voice.

EXTRA RESOURCES

Possible readings

This is not an exhaustive list, and it does not preclude reading a passage from scripture that does not specifically deal with night. An underlined reference denotes that the reading is 15 verses or more long.

Genesis 1:1-5	The creation of day and night
Genesis 1:14-19	The creation of the sun, moon and stars
Genesis 19:1-14	The threatened rape of angels
Genesis 19:30-38	Lot's daughters seduce their father
Genesis 28:10-22	Jacob's dream of a stairway to heaven
Genesis 32:22-31	Jacob wrestles with God at night
<u>Genesis 40:1-15</u>	Joseph reveals his power to interpret dreams
<u>Exodus 12:21-36</u>	The first Passover
Exodus 14:19-31	The crossing of the Red Sea
<u>Joshua 2:1-21</u>	Rahab, the prostitute, hides Hebrew spies in her workplace
<u>Judges 19:16-30</u>	The gang rape and murder of a concubine
<u>1 Samuel 26</u>	David's night-time theft of Saul's armour
2 Samuel 21:1-14	A concubine's protest moves both David and God
<u>1 Kings 3:1-15</u>	Solomon engages with God in a dream
1 Kings 3:16-28	Which of two prostitutes accidently killed her baby?
<u>Esther 6 & 7</u>	A king's troubled sleep leads to just deserts
<u>Job 38:1-19</u>	God asks the questions
Psalm 8	The night sky communicates God's wonder
Psalm 16	A night prayer of trust
Psalm 30	A psalm of despair and recovery
Psalm 42	A night prayer of puzzlement
Psalm 77	A troubled night's meditation
<u>Psalm 88</u>	A desperate night prayer for help

Appendix to Evening Liturgy 183

Psalm 91	A night psalm of reassurance
Psalm 121	A psalm of confidence
<u>Psalm 139:1-18</u>	Considering how God knows us individually
<u>Proverbs 7</u>	Twilight seduction by a prostitute
Song of Songs 3	Amorous musings in the night
Isaiah 38:9-20	A royal poem after recovery from a serious illness
Isaiah 45:1-8	God, Maker of light and darkness
Isaiah 60:1-11	A prophecy for Epiphany
Jeremiah 33:14-25	God's promise to the people is as sure as day and night
Lamentations 2:18-22	A lament for urban desolation
Jonah 4:5-11	Jonah is reprimanded for being self-pitying
Micah 3	God's condemnation of injustice and duplicity
Matthew 2:2-12	The Magi see Jesus and go home by another way
Matthew 2:13-23	Joseph's dream secures Jesus' safety
Matthew 14:22-33	Jesus walks on water at night
Matthew 25:1-13	The parable of the wise and foolish virgins
<u>Matthew 26:36-56</u>	Gethsemane and the betrayal of Jesus
Matthew 26:69-75	Peter denies Jesus
Matthew 27:55-61	The burial of Jesus
Mark 4:35-41	Jesus stills a night storm at sea
Mark 13:32-37	Being prepared, night and day
<u>Mark 14:12-31</u>	The Last Supper
<u>Luke 2:1-18</u>	The birth of Jesus and visitation of the shepherds
Luke 11:5-10	A late-night request
Luke 11:33-36	Light and darkness
Luke 12:16-21	The parable of a rich man's late-night revelation
Luke 24:28-35	The evening meal at Emmaus
John 1:1-12	Jesus as the light

John 3;1-12	Jesus' late-night visitor
John 6:16-21	Jesus walks on the sea
<u>John 13:1-17</u>	Foot-washing at an evening meal
<u>John 20:1-18</u>	Mary Magdalene meets the risen Jesus
John 20:19-23	The risen Jesus shows himself to his disciples
<u>Acts 16:16-34</u>	The effect of Paul and Silas singing at midnight
Acts 20:7-12	The boy who fell asleep
Revelation 7:11-17	A vision of the worship in heaven
Revelation 22:1-5	A vision of the fulfilment of heaven

Opening responses

Leader	In the beginning, when it was very dark, God said, 'Let there be light.'
All	**And there was light.**

(a lit candle is placed centrally)

In the beginning,
when it was very quiet,
the Word was with God.
And what God was, the Word was.

(an open Bible is placed centrally)

When the time was right,
God sent the Son.
He came among us;
he was one of us.

(a cross is placed centrally)

Closing responses

Leader	I lie down with God,
All	**and God lies down with me.**

        I lie down with Christ,
        and Christ lies down with me.

        I lie down with the Spirit,
        and the Spirit lies down with me.

        God and Christ and the Spirit –
        all three
        with me.

12A Prayers for the World and Its People

The people gather

At different times in the year prayers may be offered in the Abbey church at 2pm, for the world and its people, following this pattern.

Monday	The peace of the world
Tuesday	The care of creation
Wednesday	Economic and trade justice
Thursday	Gender and sexuality issues
Friday	Civic justice and the law
Saturday	Intercultural relations

Welcome and introduction

Opening responses

Leader   Believing that God made and loves the world,
All   **we gather.**
            That it may be reshaped to fulfil God's purposes,
            we pray.
            To seek a wisdom deeper than our own thinking,
            we listen.
            To honour God who gave us voice,
            we worship.

Chant or short song
(optional – see suggested global chants in appendix)

Theme

Leader   Today, being …day, we focus on issues associated with *(the issue is named)* and hear words which address this issue from the Bible *(or other named source)*.

Reading *(for a list of biblical readings see appendix)*

Leader   Because God's word is given to bless, inspire, comfort and disturb,
All   **thanks be to God.**

Prayers

(Three short prayers of gratitude or concern are made, each ending with)

Leader   God, in kindness,
All   **hear our prayer**

(followed by)

In this ancient place through the centuries God has heard and answered prayer.

So, if there is something we want to share with our Maker, let us do that now in the silence as God listens.

(silence)

Glory to God who created us,
to Christ who rules over the earth,
to the Spirit who dwells in our hearts
both now and for ever.
Amen.

Closing song *(optional)*

Dismissal

Leader Now go from here
and God go with you.
May Christ companion you,
the Spirit enliven you,
and may you know God's presence
today and every day.
All **Amen.**

12B Appendix to Prayers for the World and Its People

NOTES FOR THE SERVICE

At different times during the year daily prayer is offered in the Abbey, usually in the early afternoon. These prayers are kept short and will often take place as tourists are walking around the Abbey church. They are normally intercessory prayers for the world and its people. It is helpful to make an announcement ten minutes and also three minutes before the beginning of the short liturgy, inviting those who wish to participate to sit centrally. Whether many are gathered or only the leader, prayer is still offered.

Themes for the prayers

Monday	The peace of the world
Tuesday	The care of creation
Wednesday	Economic and trade justice
Thursday	Gender and sexuality issues
Friday	Civic justice and the law
Saturday	Intercultural relations

POPULAR SHORT SONGS FROM AROUND THE WORLD
... with an indication of source books where songs have been published by the Iona Community

1   ALLELUIA
    (Honduras)   CAYP

2   BE STILL AND KNOW THAT I AM GOD (x3)
    (Anon)   TIOAU

3   COME ALL YOU PEOPLE, come and praise your Maker. *(x3)*
    Come now and worship the Lord.
    (Zimbabwe)   CAYP

4   COME, BRING YOUR BURDENS TO GOD *(x3)*
    for Jesus will never say no
    (South Africa)   WWHW

5   GLORIA, GLORIA, GLORIA IN EXCELSIS DEO
    (Iona or Taizé)   CAYP

6   GLORY TO GOD, GLORY TO GOD,
    glory in the highest. *(repeated)*
    To God be glory for ever. *(rpt)*
    Hallelujah! Amen. *(rpt x3)*
    (Peru)   SBTL

7   HALLE, HALLE HALLE-LUJAH!
    (Caribbean)   M&G

8   HALLELUJAH
    (Zimbabwe)

9   HOLY, HOLY, HOLY,
    God of power and might. *(rpt)*
    Heaven and earth are full of your glory. *(rpt)*
    Hosanna, hosanna, hosanna in the highest. *(rpt)*
    Blessed is the one who comes
    in the name of the Lord. *(rpt)*
    Hosanna, hosanna, hosanna in the highest. *(rpt)*
    (Puerto Rico)

10 HOLY, HOLY, HOLY,
    my heart, my heart adores you.
    My heart is glad to say the words,
    'You are Holy, Lord.'
    (Argentina)   M&G

11 IF YOU BELIEVE AND I BELIEVE
    and we together pray,
    the Holy Spirit must come down
    and set God's people free. *(x3)*
    The Holy Spirit must come down
    and set God's people free.
    (Zimbabwe)   SBTL

12 IN THE LORD I'LL BE EVER THANKFUL
    in the Lord I will rejoice.
    Look to God and don't be afraid,
    lift up your voices, the Lord is near. *(x2)*
    (Taizé)

13 IT'S ME, IT'S ME, O LORD,
    standing in the need of prayer. *(x2)*
    (African American)

14 JESU, TAWA PANO, *(x3)*
    tawa pano, musita renyu
    JESUS, WE ARE HERE, *(x3)*
    we are here for you.
    (Zimbabwe)   M&G

15 JESUVE SARANAM. SARANAM JESUVE *(rpt)*
    (Jesus, I surrender)
    (India)   M&G

16 KNOW THAT GOD IS GOOD *(x3)*
    God is good, God is good
    (DRC)   OITB

17 LAUDATE OMNES GENTES,
    laudate Dominum. *(x2)*
    (Iona or Taizé)   CAYP

18 MAYENZIWE, 'NTANDO YAKHO *(x5)*
Your will be done on earth, O Lord. *(x5)*
(South Africa)   TIOAU

19 O LORD, HEAR MY PRAYER,
O Lord, hear my prayer:
when I call, answer me;
O Lord, hear my prayer,
O Lord, hear my prayer;
come and listen to me.
(Taizé)

Key to sources
CAYP Come All You People (Wild Goose Publications, 1995)
M&G Many and Great (WGP, 1990)
OITB One Is the Body (WGP, 2002)
SBTL Sent By the Lord (WGP, 1991)
TIOAU There Is One Among Us (WGP, 1998)
WWHW We Walk His Way (WGP 2008)

Scripture passages appropriate to themes

THE PEACE OF THE WORLD
Isaiah 2:2-4
Matthew 24:3-8
John 15:7-17
Ephesians 6:10-18
Revelation 21:1-4

THE CARE OF CREATION
Genesis 1:27-31
Job 38:1-18
Psalm 65:6-13

Isaiah 24:4-11
Jeremiah 5:20-25

ECONOMIC AND TRADE JUSTICE
Exodus 1:7-17
Jeremiah 6:11-15
Luke 12:16-26
1 Tim 6:2b-10
James 5:1-6

GENDER AND SEXUALITY ISSUES
Genesis 1:24-27
Exodus 15:15-20
Numbers 27:1-11
John 4:7-19 & 27
Galatians 3:26-29

CIVIC JUSTICE AND THE LAW
Genesis 39:6b-23
Jeremiah 32:1-15
Matthew 25:31-40
Luke 4:14-19
Acts 16:16-24

INTERCULTURAL RELATIONS
2 Kings 5:1-14
Isaiah 25:6-9
Matthew 1:2-16
Matthew 5:1-13
Luke 17:11-19

Psalms

This selection of almost fifty psalms covers the gamut of subject matter and emotional range of the Psalter. The translation is not literal, but has resulted from a careful comparison of recent English language translations married to the desire to articulate the texts in language which would be accessible to people who may not be familiar with these icons of Jewish and Christian devotion. They have also been represented in a variety of communal reading styles which, to some extent, reflect the intrinsic diversity of the original poems. Occasionally a long psalm has been shortened in the interests of communal reading.

Whether in public or private, people who read the psalms should not expect that every text will 'speak for' or 'minister to' them. The Psalms were selected and compiled to enable the people of God to have a comprehensive vocabulary of prayer which encompasses pain and distress as well as joy and faith. These are words which grounded the spirituality of Jesus; and in them – especially in the psalms of lament – we hear the pleas of the war-weary, the oppressed, the doubting, the abused and the poor who are always with us.

In Iona Abbey, the psalms are read Monday to Saturday mornings in a six-week sequence. In addition to these 'regular' psalms, a number of others have been included which are more specific to special days in the Christian calendar. This, however, does not preclude any of the psalms from being read either out of sequence or at times other than weekday morning worship.

Below is the six-week sequence and a listing of psalms and their subject matter.

WEEK	1	2	3	4	5	6
Monday	10	37	69	27	96	70
Tuesday	25	8	42	102	130	42
Wednesday	62	104	71	15	98	30
Thursday	65	18	90	139	33	103
Friday	146	23	16	84	121	150
Saturday	49	73	145	138	12	148

Psalms for specific days and seasons

Advent	8, 10, 12 & 96
Christmas	98
Epiphany	138
Lent	25, 27, 31, 42, 73, 130
Palm Sunday	122
Monday of Holy Week	8 & 84
Tuesday of Holy Week	71
Wednesday of Holy Week	70
Maundy Thursday	22 & 116
Good Friday	22 & 88
Holy Saturday	23 & 24
Easter Day	18 & 30
Easter Monday	118 & 147
Ascension	24
Pentecost	33 & 104
St Columba's Day (6th June)	34
One World Week	19 & 65

Psalms and their themes

	first line	theme
8	God, our God, how glorious is your name	creation, ecology
10	Why God? Why do you keep away?	injustice, terrorism
12	Save us, good God	deceit
15	God, who may live in your house?	Godly behaviour
16	Keep me, God	personal faith and trust
18	I love you, God. You are my strength	faith and deliverance
19	The heavens proclaim God's glory	God's creative genius
22	You who belong to God's family	gratitude
23	You, God, are my shepherd	personal faith and God's care
24	The world belongs to God	God's justice
25	God, who is good and fair	personal piety
27	God is my light	faith in the face of conflict
30	I shall praise your name to the heights	personal gratitude
31	You, O God, are my refuge	persecution
33	Shout for joy, praise God	God's purposes
34	I will bless my Maker at all times	God's kindness
37	Don't be anxious because of the wicked	affluence and privilege
42	As a deer longs for streams of cool water	depression, doubt and yearning
49	Hear this, all you nations	wealth and mortality
62	On God alone I wait silently	faith in the face of apostasy
65	You are God our deliverer	God's providence and earth's delight
69	Save me, O God. Have mercy	affliction and penitence
70	Hurry, God, and save me	pleading for help
71	My security rests in you, O God	personal faith
73	God is good to the upright	faith and its detractors
84	How lovely is your dwelling place	the joy of worship
88	O my God, I cry to you all day	deep distress
90	You, God, have been our refuge	the passing of time

first line	theme
96 Sing a new song, all the earth	God's justice and praise
98 Sing to God a new song	the praise of all creatures
102 O God, hear my prayer	personal distress
103 My soul, bless God and God's holy name	God's fidelity
104 My soul, bless God your Maker	God's providence
111 My whole heart praises God	God and justice
116 I love the Lord who listens to me	personal devotion
118 It is good to give thanks to God	God's salvation
121 If I lift up my eyes towards the hills	assurance
122 I was glad when they said to me	safe arrival
130 Out of the depths I cry to you, O God	personal distress and penitence
138 I praise you, God, with my whole heart	personal faith and hope
139 You search me, God	God's intimate care
145 I will praise your greatness, O God	God's faithfulness
146 Praise God! Praise God, O my soul.	God's comprehensive kindness
147 It is good to sing to God	God's pleasure
148 Praise God from the heavens	universal praise
150 Praise, in highest heaven	enthusiastic praise
Psalm 22 in full (for use on Maundy Thursday)	abandonment

Psalm 8

| Leader | God, our God,
how glorious is your name in all the earth;
your majesty is praised above the heavens. |
|---|---|
| **All** | **The praise on the lips of babies and children
silences those who oppose you.** |

When I look at the sky which your fingers made,
at the moon and stars you set in place,
what are humans that you should remember them,
mere mortals that you make time for them?

**Yet you have made us in your own image,
and crowned us with glory and honour.
You have appointed us guardians of creation,
and put all things under our care:**

all of them – sheep and cattle, the beasts of the field,
the birds of the air, the fish in the waters.
**God, our God,
how glorious is your name in all the earth.**

Psalm 10

| A | Why, God? Why do you keep away?
Why hide yourself when trouble strikes?
The wicked persecute the poor,
and become the cause of their misery. |
|---|---|
| B | These villains boast about what they want;
they curse God in their desire to get more.
Listen to their arrogance when they declare,
'God has forgotten who we are and what we do.' |

A	As long as they get their way, they think they will not be defeated.
B	Rise up, God, reach out your hand! Spare a thought for the victims. They commit themselves to your care; the helpless see you as their helper.
A	Defeat the power of the wicked until they can do no more evil; put an end to the trouble they cause.
B	Listen to the pleas of the innocent; hear them, give them courage. Bring justice to those who are oppressed; so that humans cause terror no more.

Psalm 12

Leader	Save us, good God, in a world without integrity where none can be trusted. People tell lies to each other; they are masters of double-speak.
All	**God bring an end to such talk and silence the tongues that brag, 'We can talk our way out of trouble; with spin we will win the day!'**

'Now I will act,' says God,
'now I will answer the prayers of the oppressed;
I have heard their cries,
I will give them the safety they long for.'

The promise of God is pure,
refined like silver and gold.
Though wickedness thrives all around,
though shamelessness meets with applause,
you, our God, will protect us,
and save us from all that we fear.

Psalm 15

Leader   God, who may live in your house?
Who may remain in your presence?

A   Whoever leads a blameless life,
and does what is right;
who speaks the truth from the heart,
whose tongue is never used for slander.

Leader   God, who may live in your house?
Who may remain in your presence?

B   Whoever does no wrong to friends,
nor spreads false rumours about neighbours;
who does not praise those God condemns,
but blesses those who serve their Maker.

Leader   God, who may live in your house?
Who may remain in your presence?

A   Whoever keeps each solemn promise
no matter what the cost;
who lends without demanding interest
and can't be bribed to hurt the innocent.

Leader   God, who may live in your house?
Who may remain in your presence?

All	**Those who behave in this way will always remain secure. They will live in God's house, they will remain in God's presence.**

Psalm 16

A	Keep me, God; with you I am safe; from you come the good things I enjoy.
B	You bless your faithful people in whose company I delight.
A	Those who run after false gods only create trouble for themselves.
B	I will never devote myself to such idols, nor even let their names cross my lips.
A	You, God, are all I want; you are food and drink for my journey.
B	You set clear boundaries for me, I am happy to live within your limits.
A	I bless God for the holy wisdom I encounter through the intimate hours of darkness.
B	With God before and God beside me nothing need shake me.
A	So my heart is glad, my soul rejoices, my body feels secure.

All	You will not let us go, O God,
	or destine us to death.
	You show us the path to life,
	your presence makes our joy complete:
	these things shall last for ever.

Psalm 18 (1-6 & 25-29)

Leader	I love you, God.
	You are my strength, my summit,
	my safe haven, my saviour.
All	You are the rock that shelters us,
	the shield that defends us,
	the tower that protects us.
	When we call to God who is worth all our praise,
	we are safe from all who threaten us.
	Once I was caught in the grip of death,
	snared by destructive forces.
	In despair I cried for help from heaven,
	and in heaven my voice was heard;
	my plea reached the ears of God.
	To the loyal, God is loyal,
	blameless to the blameless,
	pure to the pure.
	You, God, are our light,
	which lightens every darkness.
	With your help we can breach any barrier
	and scale the highest wall.

Psalm 19

All	**The heavens proclaim God's glory,** **the sky displays divine genius.**
A	Day tells its story to day, night shares its knowledge with night.
B	No speech is made, no voice is heard, yet their news is broadcast everywhere, their message goes round the world.
A	High in the sky God pitched a tent from which the sun comes out like a bridegroom from his chamber, like an athlete to her race.
B	The sun rises from one horizon; it makes a circuit to the other and nothing escapes its heat.
A	The law of God is perfect; it refreshes every soul.
B	The teaching of God is trustworthy; it helps the simple become wise.
A	The guidance of God is good; it makes the heart rejoice.
B	The commandment of God is clear; it provides light for the eyes.
A	The reverence God inspires is pure; it shall last for ever.

B	The judgements of God are true; all of them can be trusted.
All	**More to be treasured than gold, sweeter to taste than honey – such is God's wisdom and wealth.**

Psalm 22

A	You who belong to God's family, worship our only Creator.
B	God does not neglect the poor, but answers their cries for help.
A	God gives me cause for praise and inspires the vows I make.
B	The humble shall eat and be satisfied; those who search for God will give praise.
A	The ends of the earth shall remember, all races and peoples shall worship.
B	Dominion is God's alone who rules over every nation.
A	Even the dead praise their Maker; those in the grave bow their heads.
B	Those still to come will give reverence; they will speak of God's worth to their children.
A	Those yet unborn will discover that God is the One who saves us.

Psalm 23

Leader	You, God, are my shepherd; I need nothing more.
A	You let me lie down in green pastures, you lead me beside still waters; there you revive my spirit.
B	You guide me in the right paths for you are true to your name.
A	Were I to walk through the darkest valley I should not be afraid;
B	for you are at my side, your staff and crook support me.
A	You spread a table before me in clear view of my enemies.
B	You anoint my head with oil, my cup is overflowing.
All	**Unfailing goodness and kindness will follow me all my days. My home shall be in God's house as long as my life shall last.**

Psalm 24

All	**The world belongs to God:** **the earth and all its people.** **Founded on seas, surrounded by waters.**
A	Who can scale the heights to stand in God's holy presence?
B	Those whose hands and hearts are clean, who act with justice and integrity.
A	These will receive God's blessing; justice will be their reward.
B	Goodness is found by those who seek God, who serve their Maker's will.
All	**Lift up your heads, you gates!** **Stand open, you ancient doors!** **Let the King of Glory come in.**
Leader	Who is this King of Glory?
All	**God who is strong and mighty,** **whose justice defeats every evil.** **Lift up your heads, you gates!** **Stand open, you ancient doors!** **Let the King of Glory come in.**
Leader	Who is this King of Glory?
All	**None but the Lord of Hosts.** **Our God is the King of Glory.**

Psalm 25

A   God, who is good and fair,
    teaches sinners how to live.

B   God guides the humble in heart,
    and teaches them the way.

A   God's paths are marked with love and care
    for those who revere their Maker.

**All God, for the honour of your name
    pardon our guilt which is great.**

B   Those who hold God in reverence
    will be shown the path they should take.

A   They will enjoy lasting prosperity
    and their children will inherit the land.

B   God's wisdom is revealed to true worshippers;
    it is given for their instruction.

**All Our eyes are always set on God
    who can free us from every snare.**

A   Turn and show us your kindness
    when we are lonely or oppressed.

B   Relieve the trouble in our hearts
    and deliver us from distress.

A   Remember our suffering and misery
    and forgive us for our sins.

B   Take note of those who threaten us
    with violence and hatred.

A	Defend us and deliver us; be our refuge and save us from shame.
All	**Let honesty and integrity protect us, for we put our hope in you.**

Psalm 27

A	God is my light, God my salvation; of whom should I be afraid?
B	God is the stronghold of my life; why should I live in fear?
A	Should enemies try to take my life, they shall stumble and fall.
B	Should armies stand against me, still I will keep my confidence.
A	One thing I desire, this I ask of God, that I may live for ever in God's house.
B	There I would seek my Maker, and contemplate God's beauty.
A	Reveal to me your way, my God, and keep me on a level path.
B	Thus I will see your goodness at work in the land of the living.

Psalm 30

Leader   I shall praise your name to the heights
for you have lifted me up,
away from the gloating of my enemies.

A   I cried to you, God, and you healed me;
you raised me from depths of despair;
from death to life you delivered me.

B   Sing a psalm to God, you faithful people;
give thanks to God's holy name.

A   God's anger lasts for a moment,
God's grace lasts for a lifetime.

B   Tears may linger through the night,
but joy comes in the morning.

Leader   I felt secure and said to myself,
'I doubt I shall ever be shaken.'
Like a strong mountain
you protected me.

A   But then you hid your face,
and I was filled with dismay.
I cried to you, my God;
I pleaded with you for mercy:

B   What can be gained by my death,
if I disappear into oblivion?
Can dust offer heartfelt praise
or tell of your faithful love?

Leader   Hear, O God, and take pity;
come and be my helper.

All	You have turned my mourning to dancing, you have clothed me with great joy. I will sing to you without ceasing; my God, I will praise you for ever.

Psalm 31

All	**You, O God, are my refuge. Let me never be put to shame.**
A	Bend down your ear and hear me, come quickly to my rescue; be just, protect me from danger.
B	Be a place of safety for me, a rock where I find shelter; lead and guide me for your own name's sake.
All	**You, O God, are my refuge. Let me never be put to shame.**
A	Set me free from the net spread to catch me, for you are my protector. Into your hands I commit my spirit.
B	Turn your face towards me, with unfailing love defend me, do not reject me when I call your name.
A	Your goodness knows no limits; it is kept for all who revere you and turn to you in their need.
All	**You, O God, are our refuge. Let us never be put to shame.**

Psalm 33

A Shout for joy, praise God,
you who believe in justice.
Shout for joy, praise God,
you who walk in God's way.

B Tune up your instruments;
strike up the band!
Sing God new songs;
give it all you've got!

A God's word is always true,
God's work is everlasting.
God, who loves justice and fairness,
fills the whole earth with goodness.

B God's word created the heavens
and all that shines in the sky.
God set a limit for the seas
and stored their depths below.

A Let the whole earth stand in awe,
revering its mighty maker.
God spoke the world into being;
God commanded and earth appeared.

B God shatters a country's intentions,
and foils a nation's plans;
but God's intentions are constant,
heaven's purposes have no end.

A Monarchs are not saved by armies,
nor warriors by their great strength;
weapons meant for war
do not guarantee safety.

B	God's eye rests on the faithful
who hope in God's constant love
to deliver their souls from death,
and keep them alive through disaster.
All	**Our souls wait for God.
God, our help and defence.
Our hearts delight in our Maker
whose holy name we cherish.**

Psalm 34

Leader	I will bless my Maker at all times,
whose praise is forever on my lips.
All	**My soul will glorify God;
let the humble hear and rejoice.**

Together let us praise God's greatness;
together let us honour God's holy name.
**I looked for God who answered me,
bringing freedom from all my fears.**

Those who look to God become radiant,
their faces show no shame.
**God hears those who cry for help
and saves them from all their troubles.**

The angel of God keeps watch
over those who revere their Maker.
**Taste and see: God is good,
a shelter to saints and seekers.**

Hold God in awe, you holy people;
thus you will find fulfilment.

**Even if princes grow poor and hungry,
God's children shall want for nothing.**

Psalm 37

A Don't be anxious because of the wicked,
don't envy those who do wrong.
They will wither as quickly as grass,
and fade like the flowers of the field.

B Trust in God and do good;
settle down and be at peace.
Let God be your deep delight
and give you your heart's desire.

A Give your life over to God
who will bring out the best in you.
Your integrity will be clear
and as bright as the noonday sun.

B Be still in the presence of God,
calm yourself and wait patiently;
don't be jealous of those who get rich
or be vexed by those who are devious.

A Stop ranting, control your rage;
blind anger gives birth to trouble.
The wicked will be driven out;
the land will belong to the humble.

B Turn from evil, love what is good,
and you will be at peace;
God is a lover of justice
who will never abandon the faithful.

Psalm 42

A   As a deer longs for streams of cool water,
     so my heart longs for you, O God.

B   I thirst for you, the living God.
     When shall I know you are near me?

A   Tears have been my food, day and night,
     while tormenters ask, 'Where is your God?'

B   My heart breaks whenever I remember
     how I once went with others to God's house.

A   I would lead the joyful procession
     singing and shouting God's praise.

**All Why am I sunk in deep misery?
       Why am I lost and distressed?
       I shall put my hope in God,
       in the One who is my deliverer.**

A   My soul is troubled within me
     therefore I will remember you.

B   Deep calls to deep in confusion
     and all your waters sweep over me.

A   Yet by day God's love assures me;
     come night, a song leaves my lips,
     a prayer to the God of my life.

B   I ask God, 'Why have you forgotten me?'
     Why should I walk like a mourner,
     being taunted, 'Where is your God?'

All	**Why am I sunk in deep misery?**
	Why am I lost and distressed?
	I shall put my hope in God,
	in the One who is my deliverer.

Psalm 49

A	Hear this, all you nations.
	Listen all you people on earth
	both high and low, rich and poor.
B	My words contain wisdom,
	a message with meaning for you.
	Listen carefully to this proverb;
	set it to music if that helps.
A	Why should I fear in times of trouble
	when treacherous people surround me,
	made confident by their money,
	boasting in their wealth?
B	They too are mortal and must die;
	they cannot buy off their Maker.
	Such a ransom would be too high,
	beyond their power to pay.
A	We cannot guarantee our lives;
	we cannot escape the grave.
	Both wise and foolish will die,
	leaving their wealth to others.
B	Some claim land as their own,
	but a plot of ground will possess them,
	the grave their eternal home.

All	**Humans do not live for ever,** **nor do the beasts of the field.** **So, do not envy the wealthy;** **wealth is worth nothing in the grave.**

Psalm 62

All	**On God alone I wait silently:** **God my deliverer, God my strong tower.**
A	I wait silently for God, the one who will deliver me. God is my rock and my refuge ensuring that I stand firm.
B	How long will the wicked survive, beating down people with threats, as if they were fragile fences or towers waiting to be toppled?
A	They try to bring others to the ground; they delight in spreading slander. They bless with their lips but curse with their hearts.
All	**On God alone I wait silently:** **God my deliverer, God my strong tower.**
B	My safety and future lie in God who shelters me like a strong rock. Put your trust in God at all times, pour out your heart to your Saviour.
A	Mortals are merely a breath, even the powerful are an illusion.

| | Put them on scales and they rise;
their weight is lighter than air. |
|---|---|
| B | Put no trust in extortion,
or profit from ill-gotten gains.
Even though wealth may increase,
don't ever set your heart on it. |
| All | **On God alone I wait silently:
God my deliverer, God my strong tower.** |

Psalm 65

| Leader | You are God our deliverer
in whom all put their trust; |
|---|---|
| All | **All who live on earth,
all beyond the horizon.** |

By great skill and untold strength
you fixed the mountains in place;
**you calm the raging seas
and quieten the warring nations.**

People throughout the world
stand in awe of your skill.
**Lands to east and west
gratefully sing your praise.**

You care for the life of the planet,
forever tending the ground;
**you nourish the fruits of the earth,
the crops that feed your people.**

You water and level the land,
blessing each season's growth.

You crown the year with your bounty;
rich harvests are signs of your goodness.

The open pastures are lush
and hills are clothed with joy.
**The meadows are covered with sheep
and valleys burst into song.**

Psalm 69

All	**Save me, O God. Have mercy, for the floods sweep me away.**
A	Save me, O God. Come quickly, for the water has risen to my neck. Sunk in the muddy quagmire, I can barely stand.
All	**Save me, O God. Have mercy, for the floods sweep me away.**
B	I am worn out with weeping, my throat is parched and sore, Even my eyes grow weary, as I wait for you.
All	**Save me, O God. Have mercy, for the floods sweep me away.**
A	Those who hate me without cause are more than the hairs on my head; powerful and treacherous people want to end my life.
All	**Save me, O God. Have mercy, for the floods sweep me away.**

B	God, you know well that I'm foolish, and my guilt is not hidden from your sight. May none who hope in you be disgraced through me.
All	**Save me, O God. Have mercy, for the floods sweep me away.**

Psalm 70

A	Hurry, God, and save me. Come quickly, come to my aid. Confuse the devious plans of those who want to hurt me.
B	Let those intent on harming me be dishonoured and exposed. Let those who jeer and gloat be shamed into silence.
A	Sustain all those who seek you; fill them with joy and gladness. Let those who long for your help cry, 'Glory, glory to God.'
B	Meanwhile, remember me, God; I need to know you are there. Hurry to help and save me, for you are my only deliverer.
All	**God, do not delay!**

Psalm 71

Leader My security rests in you, O God;
let me never be put to shame.
All **By your saving power deliver me,
hear me and keep me safe.**

Be a rock of refuge for me
to which I can always come.
**Keep me safe from the power of the wicked,
from the grasp of the cruel and unjust**

As long as I can remember,
I have put my trust in you.
**I have leaned on you since birth,
when you brought me out of the womb.**

Keep close when energy fails me
as I spend my last years on earth.
**Let me wait in constant hope
and praise you again and again.**

Psalm 73

All **God is good to the upright,
to those who are pure in heart**

A My feet were close to slipping,
I almost lost my balance.
I had started to envy the arrogant
when I saw how the wicked flourish.

B   They seem to avoid suffering,
    their bodies are healthy and sleek;
    trouble appears to bypass them,
    their lives are free of affliction.

A   They talk with menace and malice,
    breathing down people's necks.
    They slander the kingdom of heaven
    with tongues never silent on earth

B   Many are taken in by them,
    believing they do nothing wrong.
    They say, 'Does God really care?
    Perhaps the Most High doesn't know.'

A   Have I kept myself pure for nothing,
    washing my hands in innocence?
    For every new morning brings trouble,
    and day after day I am punished.

B   Had I thought to do as they do
    I would have betrayed my people.
    So I tried to make sense of this mess,
    but found it too difficult for me.

A   Once I entered God's sanctuary
    then I began to understand.
    In a moment they will be destroyed
    on the slippery slope to ruin.

B   My God, I am always with you;
    you take me by the right hand.
    Your wisdom continues to guide me
    and you will receive me in glory.

A	Because you remember me in heaven,
	there is nothing I need upon earth.
	Though flesh and spirit may fail,
	God is my strength for ever.

All   **God is good to the upright,**
               to those who are pure in heart.

Psalm 84

All   **How lovely is your dwelling place,**
               God of power and might.

A   I long with heartfelt yearning
            to be within God's house.
            My whole being sings for joy
            to God, the living God.

B   Even the sparrow finds a home
            and the swallow makes a nest
            where she can rear her brood
            close to your holy altars.

A   Happy are those who live in your house
            forever offering praise.
B   Happy are those who trust in you
            as they walk their pilgrim way.

A   Better is one day in your temple
            than a thousand days elsewhere.
            Better to stand at the door of God's house
            than live in the tents of the wicked.

B	God is our sun, God is our shield, giver of glory and grace. God refuses no good thing to those who do what is right.
All	**Happy are those who trust in you, God of power and might.**

Psalm 88

Leader	O my God, I cry to you all day; at night I bring my prayer to you.
A	Hear me. Listen to my cry, for I have had my fill of troubles which have brought me close to the edge.
B	I am numbered among those about to die; I am like those who are beyond help, forsaken among the dead.
A	I am like the slain lying in their graves, forgotten by you completely, and cut off from your care.
B	You have plunged me into the lowest pit, into the darkest regions of the deep.
A	Your anger weighs heavily on me; I am crushed beneath its waves.
B	You have given my friends reason to avoid me; you have turned me into something repulsive.

A	I am shut in with no way out;
	my eyes are sore with weeping.
B	Every day I call to you, God;
	every day I stretch out my hands in prayer.
A	Do you perform miracles with the dead?
	Can corpses rise up to praise you?
B	Is your love proclaimed in the graveyard,
	your faithfulness known in the tomb?
A	Are your wonders performed in dark places?
	Is your justice known in the land time forgets?
B	But God, I keep crying to you;
	in the morning my prayer is offered to you.
A	Why do you reject me?
	Why do you hide your face from me?
B	I have been afflicted since childhood;
	I have endured your onslaughts. I am numb.
A	Your fury has swept over me,
	your fierce attacks have destroyed me.
B	They surround me like a flood,
	closing in on me from every side.
A	You have taken friend and neighbour far from me;
	darkness is now my only companion.

Psalm 90

All **You, God, have been our refuge
from one generation to another.**

A   Before the mountains emerged,
before the earth was born,
from everlasting to everlasting
you are God.

B   You turn back mortals to dust,
saying, 'Turn back, earth's children.'
For, in your sight, a thousand years
are like a night watch or a single day.

All **You sweep time away like a dream,
like grass that flourishes in the morning
but withers and fades come evening.**

A   We are consumed by your anger
and overwhelmed by your fury.
For you lay out our sins before you,
our secret sins are open to your gaze.

B   All our days pass under your scrutiny,
our years die away like a sigh.
We may reach the age of seventy,
perhaps eighty if we keep healthy.

A   Our years bring us struggle and sorrow.
They are soon gone and so are we.

All **Who knows the power of your anger?
Who but the faithful understand you?**

B	Help us to plan our years so that wisdom may grow in our hearts.
A	How long, O God, till you return to us? Have pity on your people.
B	Show us your love when morning breaks and we will be joyful all our days.
A	For all the days we have known misfortune, balance them with days of joy.
All	**Let your care be evident to your servants and your glory to the next generation. Let your favour rest upon us and bless the work of our hands.**

Psalm 96

All	**Sing a new song, all the earth; sing a new song to God.**
A	Sing and bless the holy name; let God's salvation be praised each day.
B	Declare God's glory among the nations, tell all people what God has done.
A	God is great, deserving of worship, worthy of praise more than worldly idols.
B	Earthly deities are custom-built, but God is the Maker of all.

All	**Sing a new song, all the earth;** **sing a new song to God.**
A	Honour and splendour belong to God in whose sanctuary are beauty and strength.
B	Give God the glory, you families of nations, offering your gifts in God's house.
A	Praise the Creator, clothed in holiness; tremble with reverence, all the earth.
B	Say to the nations, 'Our God reigns. The world is stable; it shall not be moved; God will judge it with fairness.'
All	**Sing a new song, all the earth;** **sing a new song to God.**
A	Let heaven be glad, let earth rejoice; let the sea roar and all its creatures; let the fertile fields honour their Maker.
B	Let the trees of the forest sing for joy for God is coming to judge the earth. The world shall be judged with justice, its nations judged with truth.
All	**Sing a new song, all the earth;** **sing a new song to God.**

Psalm 98

A	Sing to God a new song,
	for God has done marvellous things,
	revealing true salvation
	in the sight of all the nations
B	God has remembered the trust and care
	promised to faithful people.
	All the ends of the earth
	have seen God's saving power.
A	Sing out your joy, all the earth;
	break into songs, sing praises.
B	Praise God with the lute and harp,
	strum out beautiful melodies.
A	Praise God with trumpets and horns;
	let them make a joyful noise.
B	Let the sea and its creatures roar,
	let the world and its people shout.
A	Let the rivers clap their hands
	and the hilltops sing for joy.
All	**Praise the God who comes**
	to judge the earth with justice
	and govern its people with fairness.

Psalm 102

All **O God, hear my prayer;**
be moved by my cry for help.

A Do not hide your face
when I am in dire straits.

B Listen to my prayer;
be quick to make a response.

A My days vanish like smoke,
my body is almost burnt out.

B I wither away like grass
and forget to take any food.

A All day I groan out loud;
I am nothing but skin and bones.

B Like a desert owl in waste places,
like a lonely bird on the rooftop,
I lie awake, all alone.

A My enemies constantly taunt me;
in their rage they conspire against me.

B My bread is ashes, my drink salt tears;
you have lifted me up and thrown me aside.

A Do not leave me with my life half-lived,
you whose life lasts for ever.

B Long ago you laid the earth's foundations;
the heavens also are the work of your hands.

A	They will perish, but you endure; your years will never end.
All	**Those who serve you, and their descendants, will remain in your presence for ever.**

Psalm 103

All	**My soul, bless God and God's holy name, and do not forget God's benefits.**
A	God forgives the wrong you have done, heals you of your diseases,
B	redeems your life from the grave, crowns you with goodness and mercy,
A	keeps you with care as long as you live so your life is renewed like the eagle's.
All	**My soul, bless God and God's holy name, and do not forget God's benefits.**
A	God brings justice to those who are oppressed, as shown to Moses and his people.
B	God is gracious and merciful, slow to anger, constant in love.
A	God will not always be the accuser or keep anger hot for ever.
B	God does not deal with us as we deserve, nor punish according to our sins.

A	God's love for all faithful people
is as high and vast as the heavens.
B	As far as the east lies from the west,
God removes the wrong we have done.
All	**My soul, bless God and God's holy name,
and do not forget God's benefits.**

Psalm 104

Leader	My soul, bless God your Maker.
All	**My soul, bless God your Maker.**
Leader	God, you are magnificent,
clothed with glory and majesty,
wrapped in a cloak of light.
A	You stretch out the skies like a tent,
your home is beyond the heavens,
the clouds provide your chariot.
B	You ride on the wings of the wind.
Breezes and gales are your messengers,
fire and flames your attendants.
A	You set the earth on foundations
so firm it will never be shaken.
B	You clothed the earth with seas;
their waters covered the mountains.
A	And then you set clear limits
to safeguard the earth from flooding.

B	You supply grass for the cattle and plants for people to cultivate.
A	So good food comes from the earth, and wine to cheer our spirits.
B	How splendid are all your works, rooted in heavenly wisdom.
A	Creatures of earth and sea look to you for provision.
B	By your spirit all is created and the face of the earth is renewed.
Leader	My soul, bless God your Maker.
All	**My soul, bless God your Maker.**

Psalm 111

Leader	My whole heart praises God in the midst of the worshipping people.
A	All of God's works are great, a delight to those who study them.
B	They are full of honour and majesty, justice which lasts for ever.
A	God cares for those who show reverence, and is faithful in keeping promises.
B	All that God does is just, as are God's rules for living.

A	They are meant to endure through the ages, and be kept with faith and fairness.
B	God has redeemed the people bound to their Maker by covenant.
A	Wisdom increases when God is honoured. Trust God, find this to be true.
All	**Let God be praised for ever.**

Psalm 116

A	I love the Lord who listens to me; my prayers are heard in heaven.
B	Death and hell laid hold of me; I was desperate, distressed, and in anguish.
A	Then I called on the name of God: Save me! Save my life!
B	God is gracious and merciful; I was rescued from all that oppressed me.
A	My life was delivered from death, my eyes from tears, my feet from stumbling.
B	What shall I offer to God in return for all the grace I received?
A	I will lift the cup of salvation and call on God by name.

B	I will offer my gift of gratitude in the place beloved by God.
A	I will make my vows to my Maker in the presence of all God's people.

Palm 118

Leader	It is good to give thanks to God;
All	**God's goodness will last for ever.**
Leader	Open the gates of righteousness that I may praise my Maker.
All	**Open the gates of righteousness and let God's servant in.**
A	I thank you, for you answered me; you have become my salvation.
B	The stone that the builders rejected has become the cornerstone.
A	This is the work of God; it is marvellous in our eyes.
Leader	It is good to give thanks to God;
All	**God's goodness will last for ever.**
A	This is the day that God has made, let us rejoice and be glad in it.
B	Deliver us, God, we pray; supply our deepest needs.

A	Those who come believing are blessed in the house of God.
B	Light has shone on our darkness: celebrate this in the house of prayer.
A	You are my God, I give you thanks; offering praise and worship.
Leader	It is good to give thanks to God;
All	**God's goodness will last for ever.**

Psalm 121

Leader	If I lift up my eyes towards the hills, where can my help be found?
A	Your help comes from God, the One who made heaven and earth.
B	God will keep you from stumbling, your protector is always at hand.
A	God keeps watch over everyone and never slumbers or sleeps.
B	God is your guardian at all times, always close at hand.
A	In daytime no harm shall befall you; at night your life is secure.

B	God will guard you from evil, and protect your very soul.
All	**God watches our coming and going, now and for evermore.**

Psalm 122

Leader	I was glad when they said to me 'Let us go to the house of God.'
All	**Now we are inside the gates of Jerusalem, God's strong city.**
A	There the tribes go up, the people whom God has called.
B	They offer praise to God in the place of justice and power.
Leader	Pray for the peace of Jerusalem.
All	**Peace to all those who love you. Peace be within your walls, and safety in your streets.**
Leader	To all of those I love, my greeting is, 'Peace be with you.'
All	**For the sake of the house of God we will seek what's best for you.**

Psalm 130

Leader   Out of the depths I cry to you, O God.
Open your ears and give me a hearing.

All   **If you, O God, took note of our sins,
who could hold their head high?
But you have chosen to forgive;
and for this we revere you.**

I wait for God; I wait in hope;
my soul waits for my Maker
more than those who wait for the morning,
more than those who look for the dawn.

**Hope in God, you faithful people,
trust in God's constant love.
God's power to liberate
brings redemption from every sin.**

Psalm 138

Leader   I praise you, God, with my whole heart,
and sing in the face of earthly idols.

A   I bow down towards your holy temple
and praise your love and faithfulness,
for you have raised your name and word
above all other things.

Leader   On the day I called, you answered me
and made me bold and strong.

B   All earth's monarchs shall worship you
when they hear what you have to say.

	They shall tell of what you have done,
	for your glory is great beyond measure.

A	Though you are above all,
	you care for the humblest of folk,
	while the proud are kept at arm's length.

B	Should I be confronted with trouble,
	you will preserve my life;
	your outstretched hand will deliver me.

All	**Your purpose will be fulfilled in us,**
	for your love shall last for ever.
	Safeguard those your hands have made.

Psalm 139

A	You search me, God, and you know me;
	you know my resting and my rising;
	you discern my thoughts from afar.

B	You are familiar with all my ways –
	where I go, what I do –
	and you know every word before I say it.

A	Your presence is all around me;
	you lay your hand upon me.

B	Such knowledge is too wonderful for me;
	it is beyond my understanding.

A	Is there anywhere I could I go
	where you were not there before me?

B	If I climb up to heaven, you are there;
	if I bed down in hell, there I meet you.

A	If I took the wings of the morning and lived beyond the horizon, even there your hand would find me, your right hand would hold me fast.
B	If I asked the darkness to cover me and the daylight turned to night, the darkness would not be dark to you; night would be bright as day.
A	Search me, O God, and know my heart; test me and know my thoughts.
B	Prevent me from doing what offends you, and lead me in the everlasting way.

Psalm 145

Leader	I will praise your greatness, O God; I will bless your name for ever.
A	Every day I will praise you and honour your name without ceasing.
B	God, you are great and deserve our praise; your glory is beyond our understanding.
A	Each generation shall speak of your worth and celebrate your goodness.
B	I will meditate on your wonderful work and consider what you have done.
A	God is gracious and merciful, slow to anger and constant in love.

B	God's goodness and compassion are meant for all creation.
A	God keeps every promise, God's ways are always gracious.
B	God lifts up those who are falling and raises those bowed down.
A	All eyes look to you, O God, who supplies every creature's need.
B	God, whose ways are just and kind, draws near to all believers.
All	**Our mouths will sing out praise. God's name be blessed for ever.**

Psalm 146

Leader	Praise God! Praise God, O my soul! As long as I live I'll sing praise to my Maker.
A	Do not put your trust in human leaders, in mortals who cannot save you.
B	When they stop breathing, they return to the earth; on that day their plans perish.
A	Those whose joy knows no bounds find their help and their hope in God.
B	God made the heavens and the earth, the seas and all they contain.
A	God keeps faith, deals out justice, and gives food to the hungry.

B	God sets the prisoners free and opens the eyes that are blind.
A	God lifts up those who have fallen and loves those who practise goodness.
B	God cares deeply for the stranger, supports the widowed and orphaned, and ruins the schemes of the wicked.
All	**Praise God who rules for ever, from generation to generation.**

Psalm 147

All	**It is good to sing to God to offer heartfelt praise.**
A	God builds up Jerusalem and gathers exiled people.
B	God heals the broken-hearted and binds up all their wounds.
A	God lifts the hurt and fallen and throws the wicked to the ground.
B	God decides the number of stars; giving each one its name.
A	Great and powerful is God whose wisdom none can fathom
All	**It is good to sing to God to offer heartfelt praise.**

B	Sing songs of gratitude to God
and play a beautiful melody.
A	God covers the sky with clouds
to water and nourish the earth.
B	God provides food for the animals
and answers the young raven's cry.
A	God delights in the humble reverence
of those who trust in God's love.
All	**It is good to sing to God
to offer heartfelt praise.**

Psalm 148

A	Praise God from the heavens,
praise God in the highest of heavens.
B	Praise God, all you angels,
all you who live in God's presence.
A	Praise God, sun and moon
and all you glittering stars.
B	Praise God above the skies
in the realms beyond our knowledge.
A	Praise God from the earth,
sea monsters and ocean depths.
B	Praise God, fire and frost, snow and hail,
winds that blow at God's command.
A	Praise God, mountains and hills,
orchards and great forests.

B	Praise God, all animals, tame and wild, creatures that creep and birds that fly.
A	Praise God, every nation, those who rule and those who judge.
B	Praise God, men and women alike, youth and old together.
A	Let them praise and honour God's name, whose glory abounds for ever.
All	**Let those who are close to God respond in generous praise!**

Psalm 150

Leader	Praise, in highest heaven, the One who made the earth.
A	Praise God's wonderful deeds; praise God's excellent greatness.
B	Praise God with the blast of the trumpet and the strumming of the guitar.
A	Praise God with rhythm and dancing, fiddles, drums and flutes.
B	Praise God with clanging cymbals, the louder they clash the better!
All	**Let everything that breathes praise God. Hallelujah! Hallelujah! Hallelujah!**

Psalm 22 *(complete version for Maundy Thursday)*

Leader	My God, my God, why have you forsaken me? I cry desperately for help but still it does not come.
A	During the day I call out and yet you do not answer. I call at night but get no rest.
B	Yet you are enthroned as the Holy One, the object of Israel's praises.
A	Our ancestors put their trust in you; they trusted and you saved them.
B	They called to you and escaped from danger; they believed and were not disappointed.
A	No longer human, I am a worm, despised and scorned by everyone.
B	All who see me jeer at me; they stick out their tongues, shake their heads and say
A	'You relied on God. Why haven't you been saved? Has God forsaken a favourite?'
B	It was you who brought me through birth; when a baby, you kept me safe.
A	I have relied on you since I was born; you have always been my God.
B	Do not keep away from me! Trouble is here and no one to help me out.

A	Enemies surround me like bulls,
	fierce bulls from fertile pastures.
B	They open their mouths like lions,
	determined to tear me apart.
A	My strength has all but abandoned me
	like water spilt on the ground.
B	My bones are out of joint,
	my heart has melted like wax.
A	My throat is as dry as plaster,
	my tongue sticks to my mouth;
	you have left me to die in the dust.
B	A gang of villains surrounds me,
	like a pack of dogs they close in on me,
	tearing my hands and my feet.
A	They stare at my withered body;
	my bones are there to be counted.
B	They divide my possessions among them
	and gamble for all my clothes.
A	O God, don't stay away from me!
	Come quickly! Come to my rescue!
B	Save me from being slaughtered!
	Save my life from these dogs!
A	Rescue me from these lions;
	I am helpless before these wild bulls.

B	I will declare the help you give me; I will praise your name in public.
A	You who belong to God's family, worship our only Creator.
B	God does not neglect the poor, but answers their cries for help.
A	God gives me cause for praise and inspires the vows I make.
B	The humble shall eat and be satisfied; those who search for God will give praise.
A	The ends of the earth shall remember, all races and peoples shall worship.
B	Dominion is God's alone who rules over every nation.
A	Even the dead praise their Maker; those in the grave bow their heads.
B	Those still to come will give reverence; they will speak of God's worth to their children.
A	Those yet unborn will discover that God is the One who saves us.
Leader	I will strike the shepherd and the sheep will be scattered.

Chants

Alleluia (South Africa)

Melody © copyright control

Come, bring your burdens to God

Words & melody: South African traditional, from the singing of the Mooiplaas congregation. Arrangement: Welile Sigabi, South Africa, transcribed by Barbara Clark, Mairi Munro & Martine Stemerick.

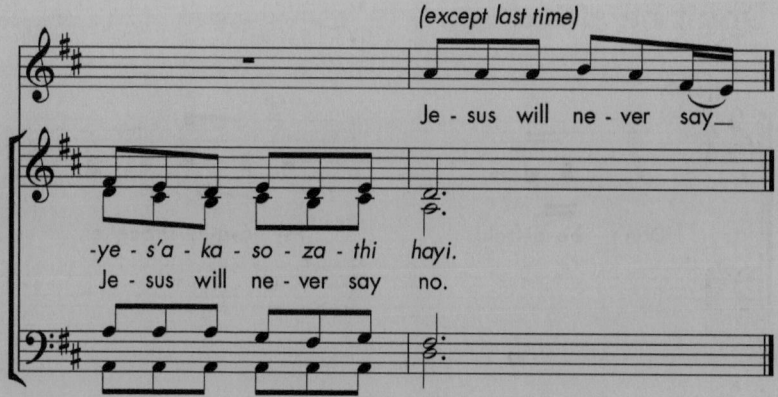

Words and melody: South African traditional. Arrangement © copyright control.
Words and melody: South African traditional, from the singing of the Mooiplaas congregation. Arrangement: Welile Sigabi, South Africa, transcribed by Barbara Clark, Mairi Munro and Martine Stemerick.

Dona nobis pacem

Words: trad. liturgical

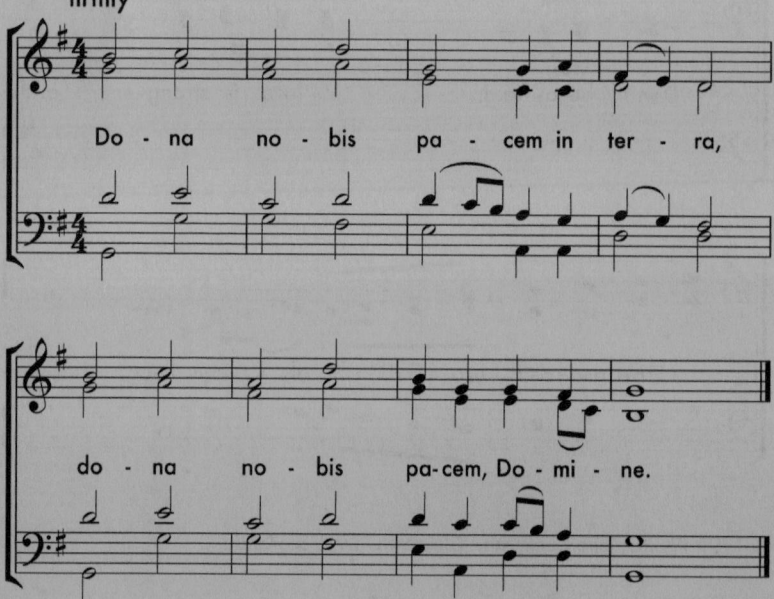

Music © 1995 WGRG, Iona Community, Glasgow G5 9JP, Scotland

Don't be afraid

© 1995 WGRG, Iona Community, Glasgow G5 9JP, Scotland

God to enfold you

Words and Music © 1997 WGRG, Iona Community, Glasgow G5 9JP, Scotland

Kyrie eleison (Guatemala)

Words: liturgical traditional.
Melody: Guatemalan original, source unknown; transcribed by Mairi Munro.

Arrangement © 2008 WGRG, Iona Community, Glasgow G5 9JP, Scotland

Kyrie eleison (El Salvador)

Words: liturgical traditional.
Melody: William Ramirez.

Melody © copyright control

Lord Jesus Christ, lover of all

© 1987 WGRG, Iona Community, Glasgow G5 9JP, Scotland

On God alone I wait silently

Words: from Psalm 62

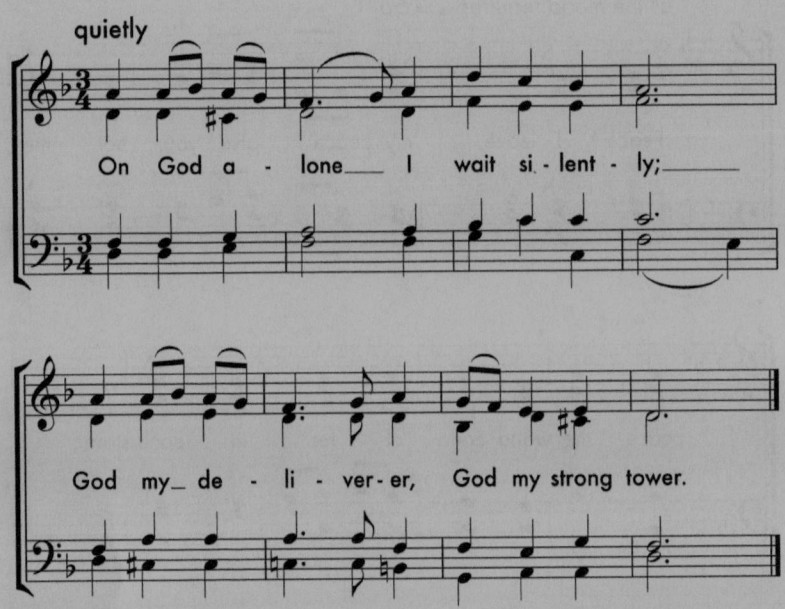

Paraphrase and Music © 1993 WGRG, Iona Community, Glasgow G5 9JP, Scotland

Peace, I leave

Paraphrase (John 14:17)

Paraphrase and Music © 2012 WGRG, Iona Community, Glasgow G5 9JP, Scotland

Take, O take me as I am

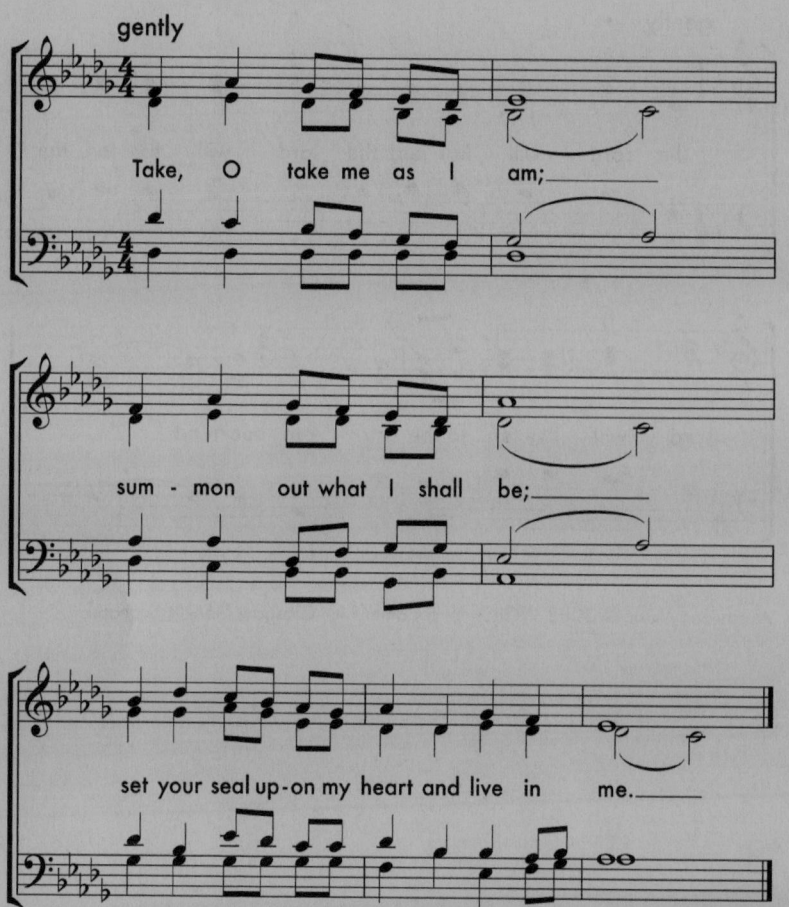

© 1995 WGRG, Iona Community, Glasgow G5 9JP, Scotland

The Lord will listen

Words and Music © 2008 WGRG, Iona Community, Glasgow G5 9JP, Scotland

Through our lives and by our prayers

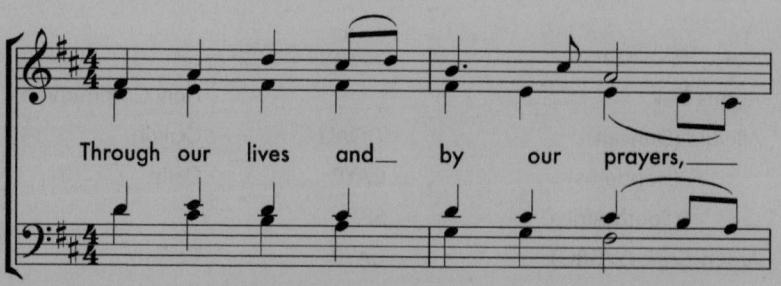

Words and Music © 1987 WGRG, Iona Community, Glasgow G5 9JP, Scotland

Short songs suggested for the liturgies,
with sources where published by the Iona Community

Song & origin	Source book	Liturgy
Agnus Dei		Holy Communion
Alleluia (Duncan)	TIOAU	Ceilidh
(Honduras)	CAYP	Daily
(South Africa)	SBTL	
Amen Celtic (WGRG)	CAYP	Ceilidh
Themba (S. Africa)	WWHW	Ceilidh
Ameni (S. Africa)	TIOAU	Ceilidh
Amen Siakudumisa (S. Africa)	M&G	Ceilidh
Be Still and Know (WGRG)	TIOAU	Daily
Come all you people (Zimbabwe)	CAYP	Healing
Come to me (WGRG)	WWHW	Healing
Don't be afraid (WGRG)	TIOAU	Healing
Gloria in Excelsis (Iona trad.)	CAYP	Welcome
		Daily
(Taizé)		Welcome
		Daily
Glory to God (Peru)	SBTL	Daily
God welcomes all (S. Africa)	WWHW	Welcome
Halle, halle, halle (Caribbean)	TIOAU	Ceilidh
		Daily
Hallelujah (Zimbabwe)		Daily
Holy, Holy, Holy (Puerto Rico)		Daily
Holy, Holy, Holy (Argentina)	M&G	Daily
If you believe (Zimbabwe)	SBTL	Daily
In the Lord I'll be ever … (Taizé)		Welcome
		Daily
It's me, O Lord (Afric/Amer)		Daily
Jesu Tawa Pano (Zimbabwe)	M&G	Daily
Jesus we are here for you (Zimb.)	M&G	Daily
Know that God is good (DCR)	OITB	Welcome
		Daily

Kyrie Eleison		Holy Communion
(Ghana)	M&G	Healing
Bridget (WGRG)	TIOAU	Healing
(Ukraine)	M&G	Healing
Laudate Omnes Gentes (WGRG)	CAYP	Daily
(Taize)		Daily
Lord, draw near (WGRG)	TIOAU	Healing
Lord Jesus Christ, lover … (WGRG)	TIOAU	Healing
Lord of Life we come (Scotland)	TIOAU	Healing
Mayenziwe (South Africa)	TIOAU	Ceilidh
		Daily
Mungu Ni Mwema (DCR)	OITB	Welcome
		Daily
O Lord, hear my prayer (Taizé)		Daily
Sanctus		Holy Communion
Sizohamba Naye (S. Africa)	OITB	Ceilidh
Ubi Caritas et Amor (Taizé)		Healing
We will walk with God (S. Africa)	OITB	Ceilidh
Yesuve Saranam (India)	M&G	Daily
Your will be done on earth (S. Africa)	TIOAU	Ceilidh
		Daily

Key to sources

CAYP Come All You People (Wild Goose Publications, 1995)
HSNW Heaven Shall Not Wait (WGP, 1989)
M&G Many and Great (WGP, 1990)
OITB One Is the Body (WGP, 2002)
SBTL Sent By the Lord (WGP, 1991)
TIOAU There Is One Among Us (WGP, 1998)
WWHW We Walk His Way (WGP 2008)

Concerning worship

The services in this book reflect important aspects of what the Iona Community believes about worship.

We owe our very existence as a community to the central Gospel conviction that worship is all that we are and all that we do. Either everything we do is an offering to God, or nothing. We may not pick and choose.

Our whole life, we believe, is a search for wholeness. We desire to be fully human, with no division into the 'sacred' and the 'secular'. We desire to be fully present to God, who is fully present to us, whether in our neighbour or in the political and social activity of the world around us, whether in the field of culture or of economics, and whether in prayer and praise together or in the very centre and soul of our being.

Of ourselves we cannot make this happen. We cannot make ourselves whole any more than we can make ourselves happy or good. But we do believe that by grace we are to structure our lives, both individually and together, in obedience to the vision that God has given us of what wholeness is like, primarily through the life, death and resurrection of Jesus Christ.

So, on Iona, we are committed to the belief that worship is everything we do, both inside and outside the church. We begin each day with prayer together, common prayer, for we are a community, given to each other by God. In the morning service we do not end with a benediction, but simply with responses that prepare us to go straight out to the life of the world, there to continue worship in the context of our work. In the evening we come together again for common prayer, but we do not begin the service with a call to worship, for we have been at worship all day long. And only in the evening service do we have a final benediction at the close of the day.

In this symbolic way we try to express our conviction that the whole of our day is all of a piece, bracketed with common prayer, but continuing throughout every action of work, common life and recreation as one liturgy, one work of service offered to God.

On Iona, our common life is fed from many sources. The past is all around us. We are the inheritors of the Celtic tradition, with its deep sense of Jesus as the head of all, and of God's glory in all of creation. So we use prayers from the Celtic Church for welcome, for work, and in expressing the needs of the world. We are the inheritors of the Benedictine tradition, with its conviction that 'to work is to pray', its commitment to hospitality, and its sense of order, all reflected in our services and our lifestyle. And we are the inheritors of the tradition of the Reformers, with their evangelical zeal, their call to commitment, and their deep understanding of the continuing challenge to every generation to find 'new ways to touch the hearts of all'. All this, we hope, you will find in how we pray and work on Iona.

Because we are an ecumenical community, we also draw on many modern Christian traditions in our services. This is a great privilege for us, and something we value very highly. It also reminds us that our life and our services here are no 'hole in the corner' affair. All we are and all we do, our work and our prayer, are part of the ongoing prayer and work of the whole Church in heaven and on earth: we are part of the one communion of saints.

A time on Iona often changes people. God has clearly used this place very powerfully over the centuries. The Iona Community does not believe that we are brought here to be changed into 'religious' people, but rather to be made more fully human. Our common life, including our services, is directed to that end.

In the words of the German martyr Dietrich Bonhoeffer, we believe that 'the Christian is not a religious person, but simply a human being, as Jesus was a human being, profoundly this-worldly, characterised by discipline, and the constant knowledge of death and resurrection'.

The Iona Community

Founded in 1938 by Revd George MacLeod, a visionary Scottish Presbyterian, the Iona Community is an ecumenical Christian movement committed to seeking new ways of living and expressing the Gospel in today's world. George MacLeod felt called to rebuild the substantial living quarters and ancillary buildings of Iona Abbey, a Benedictine building which had been destroyed at the Reformation. The Abbey, the cathedral church of which had been rebuilt by the Duke of Argyll, occupies the site where St Columba began his mission to Scotland in 563AD.

The initial intention was for the reconstructed Abbey to house an ecumenical seminary. Instead the Abbey (and subsequently the MacLeod Centre) became places attracting people from all walks of life to live in community together as guests, for weeks of reflection and engagement, or for longer periods as volunteers and staff.

The present Community has over two hundred and forty members, around fifteen hundred Associates and an equal number of Friends. Members do not normally live on Iona except when employed as staff. Being part of a dispersed community, they live throughout the British Isles and abroad. They come from a variety of backgrounds and represent a wide spectrum of church tradition. They are bound together by a rule of life and faith to which all make an annual recommitment. The Rule includes:

- Daily prayer, regular engagement with scripture and public worship.
- Working for justice, healing and peace locally, nationally and internationally.
- Meeting together for mutual encouragement, and accounting to each other for the use of time, money and resources.
- Sharing in the corporate life and organisation of the Community.

While members are expected in their own lives to work for social and political change, and for the renewal of the church, the Community engages in discussion and action on specific matters of common concern. These currently include:

- The promotion of peace and justice through opposing nuclear arms and seeking a reduction in the arms trade.
- Identifying the causes of poverty and marginalisation and supporting the cause of the poor, the exploited and refugees.
- Encouraging ecumenical cooperation and creative worship in the life of the churches.
- Affirming the equality before the law of LGBT people and enabling inclusion where they have been excluded.
- Caring for creation by encouraging personal and collective accountablity for use of energy.
- Developing new initiatives in youth work.

At the Community's three residential centres – the Abbey and the MacLeod Centre on Iona, and Camas Outdoor Centre on the Ross of Mull – guests are welcomed during the season that runs from March to October, and over Christmas. The centres are run by a resident group of about twenty-five people, including several Community members, assisted by around thirty volunteers from all over the world. The Abbey, Macleod Centre and Camas can offer hospitality to over a hundred people each week. There is a unique opportunity to extend horizons and forge new relationships by sharing with staff and other guests an experience of the common life in worship, work, discussion and relaxation. Programmes focus on themes relating to the concerns of the Community. The Community also has a shop on Iona, just outside the Abbey grounds, which carries an attractive range of books and craft goods.

The Community's administrative headquarters are in Glasgow, which also serves as a base for work with young people, the Wild Goose Resource Group working in the field of worship, a bi-monthly magazine, *Coracle*, and a publishing house, Wild Goose Publications. Between Glasgow, Iona and Camas the Community now has a staff of almost fifty people.

For information about the Iona Community:
The Iona Community, Suite 9, Fairfield, 1048 Govan Road,
Glasgow G51 4XS, Scotland
t: +44 (0)141 429 7281
e: admin@iona.org.uk
w: www.iona.org.uk

For enquiries about visiting Iona:
Iona Abbey, Isle of Iona, Argyll PA76 6SN, UK
t: +44 (0)1681 700404
e: ionacomm@iona.org.uk
w: www.iona.org.uk/island-centres/the-abbey/
  www.iona.org.uk/island-centres/macleod-centre/

For enquiries about visiting Camas:
Camas Centre, Ardfenaig, Bunessan, Isle of Mull PA67 6DX, UK
t: +44 (0)1681 700367
e: camas@iona.org.uk
w: www.iona.org.uk/island-centres/camas/

For information about Wild Goose Publications:
Wild Goose Publications
t. +44 (0)141 429 7281
e: admin@ionabooks.com
w: www.ionabooks.com

For information about the Wild Goose Resource Group:
Wild Goose Resource Group
t. +44 (0)141 429 7281
e: wgrg@iona.org.uk
w: www.wildgoose.scot

Books about the Iona Community

Chasing the Wild Goose
The story of the Iona Community
Ron Ferguson

The history of the Iona Community including St Columba's founding of an influential Celtic Christian community on the Hebridean island of Iona in the sixth century; the work of George MacLeod whose inspiration placed Iona firmly on the Christian map once again in the twentieth century; and the current broad span of the Community with its concerns for spirituality, politics, peace and justice.

Living by the Rule
The Rule of the Iona Community
Kathy Galloway

A series of reflections on living by the Rule of the Iona Community. As the church becomes polarised in many places, people are seeking a committed life which is radical, but also open, ecumenical and inclusive. Such resources as are found in the Community's Rule give an anchor which works against the grain of suspicion, and states that there are alternatives, that a Christian life can be lived fully in ways which do not have, by definition, to be either right-wing or reactionary.

George MacLeod
Founder of the Iona Community
Ron Ferguson

The definitive biography of one of the twentieth century's most fascinating and influential churchmen, an outspoken challenger to the status quo and the founder of the radical and often controversial Iona Community.

Outside the Safe Place
An oral history of the early years of the Iona Community
Anne Muir

In 2004, the Iona Community became concerned that many of the people who could bear witness to its early days were by then in their 70s or 80s. As a result, they commissioned an oral history project, so that their testimonies would not be lost. This book is based on the recordings of their stories.

Iona: God's Energy
The vision and spirituality of the Iona Community
Norman Shanks

The author shows how the Community, in its work on Iona and elsewhere, has developed an integrated vision rooted in everyday living. It is committed to peace-making and action on social issues; the breaking down of barriers between those of different faiths and styles of faith; and the development of new, relevant ways to worship.

A Pilgrim's Guide to Iona Abbey
Chris Polhill

A guidebook with colour photographs that takes you around the church and cloisters of Iona Abbey, giving you background information on the main features and providing suggestions for reflection and prayer at each point. Also included are some stories about the Abbey and life in community from Iona Community members.

Around a Thin Place
An Iona Pilgrimage guide
Jane Bentley & Neil Paynter

A full-colour guide to the Iona Pilgrimage, both off-road and on-road, including a rich collection of readings, prayers, poems, photographs, songs, stories and reflections. Island visitors and armchair pilgrims alike are invited to take a prayerful, perhaps life-changing, journey around what George MacLeod, the Founder of the Iona Community, described as a 'thin place' – only a tissue paper separating the material from the spiritual.

For these and more books, e-books, CDs
and digital downloads, visit

www.ionabooks.com